Couple's Answers for Cancer

How to fight and defeat cancer while living a joyful life

Couple's Answers for Cancer

How to fight and defeat cancer while living a joyful life

by
Larry and Shelly Bevis

iUniverse, Inc.
New York Bloomington

iUniverse books may be ordered through booksellers or by contacting:

iUniverse
1663 Liberty Drive
Bloomington, IN 47403
www.iuniverse.com
1-800-Authors (1-800-288-4677)

Because of the dynamic nature of the Internet, any Web addresses or links contained in this book may have changed since publication and may no longer be valid. The views expressed in this work are solely those of the author and do not necessarily reflect the views of the publisher, and the publisher hereby disclaims any responsibility for them.

ISBN: 978-1-4401-5072-2 (sc)
ISBN: 978-1-4401-5071-5 (ebook)

Printed in the United States of America

iUniverse rev. date: 06/25/2009

Table of Contents

Preface

Upon reviewing available material for couples we found many books written by cancer survivors and professionals but few from a couple's point of view. The purpose of this book is to provide hope, inspiration and information to couples dealing with cancer. Without question, I would have died after my first surgery without my wife. We are motivated to write this book due to having friends and acquaintances suffer from lack of understanding and support while living with cancer, my wife Shelly, whom I affectionately call Wildflower, and I were working in our tax and accounting business. In the last year we invested into a franchise tax business, opened an office, quit our safe jobs, hired a staff and started to specialize in income tax returns and business accounting.

—Larry Bevis

Then Cancer dropped in..........

Chapter 1:
CANCER DROPS IN

Larry's Story

While taking a walk late one evening in October Shelly saw that I was dragging my left foot. I finally agreed to see the doctor only because she insisted. I was actually irritated that I had to go to the Doctor and get an MRI, I felt as if there was nothing wrong with me. I was never sick and had to pay the $1,000 deductible for the MRI. I felt that I was wasting my money to have a procedure that I didn't need. Boy was I wrong! According to the MRI the cancer was about the size of half a banana, it was malignant and it was serious. A biopsy was scheduled within the week, to identify the type of tumor it was. I have BRAIN CANCER! I have a brain tumor, an Ana plastic Astrocytoma Grade III. My doctor saw the MRI in November and said that left untreated I would die within a month. With surgery I could live from three months if things didn't go well and up to three years if the treatments worked as they should. I had just been told the worst thing that could happen next to loosing Shelly or my life. I believe I owe my survival to my wife, doctors and faith. I have BRAIN CANCER!

Shelly's Story

It was a normal Thursday. Larry had been to the doctor, and he was scheduled for an MRI at 3 p.m. When he wasn't home by five, I began to worry. Then the phone rang at 5:05 and the doctor told me he was sending Larry home to get me and to come back to his office and to go to the back door of the clinic and knock, the clinic was closed and he was waiting for us, that was my first clue that things were going to be bad. Dr. Long said that I should drive back to the office, and that he needed to speak with both of us as soon as possible. As I waited on the porch for Larry to return home I knew that something was wrong, that the news was not going to be good. How bad it turned out to be was a complete shock to me. The doctor flipped the MRI image up on the backlit screen and said "These types of brain tumors" and the rest just faded into gibberish. The only words I heard over and over were "brain tumor." Life had changed in less than a minute. We walked out of the office, got into the car and drove home. Larry did not want to talk about it until we saw the neurologist the next day. Needless to say we didn't sleep much that night; we would not know the full extent of what we were dealing with until 1 p.m. the following day. The neurologist waiting room was very elegant; it struck me as not being the type of place where you would receive bad news. How bad the news could be delivered was also a complete shock to me. The neurologist was callous and very curt. I understand that these doctors are highly trained and have spent the bulk of their lives in school but I wonder, what is the point of being a brilliant neurologist if you forget that your patients are humans that have feelings? The way he treated Larry was extremely upsetting. In fact it was unacceptable. I finally ended up firing this neurologist as he was so negative, making comments like "I wouldn't touch it with a ten-foot pole, and asking, "Why would you want a section sent out for a second opinion?" and basically, his arrogant attitude. I realized I didn't have to put up with this snot so I fired him. The first visit, he told Larry he would never work at his business again and said he wanted to put Larry in the hospital to do a biopsy to determine the tumor type and grade. Larry said he needed to think about it; I pleaded with him to go. I even took him by his general physician to talk with him about the biopsy. In the end his mother told him he could not come home for Thanksgiving because he had to go to the hospital. He went in on a Saturday due to the massive brain swelling for a biopsy on Monday. What a terror-filled weekend. I watched Larry lay there not knowing where he was or why he was there or what was happening except it was bad.

LARRY'S TIP:

You need someone who can help and support you. Someone who will fight with you and help keep things together until the dust settles.

SHELLY'S TIP:

Tell your spouse that you love and value them and that you will get through this together.

COUPLE'S TIP:

Remember that terrible news is traumatic and a shock to the mind and body. Don't panic no matter how bad the news appears to be, as you have to spend some quiet time together to talk about your feelings, concerns and worries. The communication has to be wide open. Faith is defined as the belief of something unseen. Look hard at faith, your beliefs and how you want to handle the news. Toss it all out, you have nothing to lose, next to death you have just been given the worse news possible. Being truthful and honest with each other will actually make you stronger and not as scared. There are words in the human language that strike fear in the hearts of all, Death, Heart Attack, and Cancer. These things happen to other people but alas my friends; no one can predict when any of these events will enter your life and become very personal to you. We held each other and cried and then wiped our tears and started talking about how we were feeling and what avenues we wanted to take. Two things we decided very quickly, we would strengthen our faith and we would handle this with grace and turn the negative into a positive. We want to be inspirational to people. We want to give hope.

Chapter 2:
THE OPERATION

Larry's Story

December, about half of the cancer was removed during the first operation. When I returned home from Moffitt Cancer Center I was in very poor condition. I was thankful for my next-door neighbor, Bill Pearce, to help Shelly get me into the house. I had no control over any of my body functions including standing up. I lived in a semiconscious state for the next eight days. Shelly watched over me and on the fifth day she said that I opened my eyes and said, "I am just going to die, it is too hard to do this and live through it." She then told me that my parents were on their way from Illinois and that I could not die until they got here on Tuesday. I recall none of the eight days; Shelly told me that she stayed awake at night sitting next to me on the bed telling me to come back to the sound of her voice. I remember none of this. My brother Kevin helped my parents come to Florida. My sister Jennice and her husband Larry came from Chicago, and Kevin and his wife Arlene came from St. Paul Minnesota. On the eighth day after surgery I woke up and could get a grip on what was happening and was so happy to have my family around me. Mom and Dad were a welcome sight. Shelly said that I had called her Julie when I got home for the first three days when I did mumble something and try to talk. I did not know anyone by the name of Julie at that time. Shelly also hired a home health aide to come and help her, as I had to learn to walk and balance again. The home health aide came one day and never returned again. I guess I was too much trouble. Early on many friends came to visit but Shelly held most of them back. I had no control over myself and I did not want to be seen by my friends in such a state. My neighbor Bill Pearce and people from the church helped us with any and everything that we needed. Our friends Greg and Judy Conn were a Godsend. They could not do enough and the support is comforting. You know that people care. My parents stayed from December 11 through January 16 and worried most of the time.

Shelly's Story

The surgery was a nightmare for me. They took Larry back at 10:00 a.m., and I didn't see the doctor until almost 6:00 that night. My daughter drove over to be with me. I also had friends in Tampa and they also waited with us. They did a great job in keeping my mind occupied through the long, scary day. I prayed a lot. There are things they don't tell you when you take a brain surgery person home like how much swelling will occur and how each individual will recover. Larry was great the day after surgery and they discharged him home at 3 p.m. from ICU. The following day and days to come were just the opposite. By the time we arrived home on Wednesday after surgery on Monday Larry could not even walk nor was he fully conscious. I called our next-door neighbor Bill Pearce to help me get Larry into the house and we put him in his recliner and he just lay there. Later that night I got him moved into the bed, liners on the bed and diapers on him. I was glad he was not conscious to know all of this. I watched over him carefully for the next eight days as he lapsed in and out of consciousness. I cried and prayed and worried that I would never see my husband again. On the fifth day Larry opened his eyes looked at me and calmly said "Shelly I am going to close my eyes and die, this is too hard" I responded by telling him that his parents were coming down to see him and they could not travel all that way and find him dead. I made him promise me that he would stay alive until his parents arrived. I was once again, breathlessly scared, I just felt numb and alone. I called Larry's brother Kevin and told him what I had told Larry and he made the arrangements for Larry's parents to fly down. The morning they were to arrive, Larry opened his eyes and said, "I feel so much better." I exhaled. I did not realize that I had been holding my breath for days wondering what was going to happen and trying to keep the positive energy and faith alive.

I was immediately exhausted. Larry's brother and his wife Arlene, his sister Jennice and her husband Larry also drove the many miles from St. Paul and Chicago to be here with us. The positive family support was like a booster shot for Larry. The church was also a powerful support for us during this time. Larry's uncle had come from Louisiana along with his wife and daughter to be with us until the rest of the family arrived. Word got out that we were home, that the family was coming, and that we needed help and food. Uncle George said that the doorbell started ringing at 4 p.m. and the parade of cars, food and people went on for hours. He said he could not even sit down between the people coming to deliver food and comforting words and many much needed prayers; he shook his head and said, "I have never seen anything like it."

LARRY'S TIP:

I don't remember much about this time after the surgery. I tried not to panic, or be scared as I felt I was doing something positive to fight the tumor. I wanted as much of it cut out as possible, you will too. Don't panic about dying, there is nothing you can do except to pray, talk to your god and cannel all of your energy into positive thoughts about the cancer being cut out.

SHELLY'S TIP:

You must step up now and take charge of your spouse, their health and their outlook as they will react the way you act. You must claim out loud that you will fight with everything you have to keep your spouse healthy and with you.

COUPLE'S TIP:

Don't waste time and energy asking why, why me, why us, don't waste energy being scared and depressed. We all know that you can react to news either positively or negatively. Positive thinking and actions are by far the best choice. If you let your mind consider defeat you will lose the battle. We don't want to sound like Pollyanna here but we know from experience that positive days and positive actions beat the negative any day of the week. Hold onto each other; don't be scared, there are better days ahead. Someone who had cancer once said that "you get used to it," when I heard this I thought are you nuts? He was dead on, you do get used to it and it is up to you how you deal with the journey that lies ahead.

Chapter 3:
CONFRONTING CANCER

Larry's Story

Confronting the cancer is a life-or-death situation. This means that dealing with the tumor is the first job the two of you have. People have jobs and have to work. We owned a tax and accounting business and every day for weeks we would get up, go to chemotherapy and then drive the 18 miles to the business and work there from noon until closing at 9 p.m. We could not afford to pay our employees to stay until closing so we were at the business alone every day, six days a week from 5 p.m. until closing at nine. We also worked most Saturdays until mid-season by ourselves. I would lie on the couch in the back room so sick and so fatigued that I could not get up and Shelly would run the business. We knew that we would have to sell the business, as Shelly could not run it alone and take care of me. We were unsure if I could ever return to work again. It would be a miracle to sell a tax business during tax season. Luckily, we sold the business within two weeks of deciding to sell. We were giving up our income but we knew that if we wanted to fight the tumor we would have to give it our all. Even with good health insurance we have spent close to $100,000 out of pocket between eight-hour car trips to the cancer center every six weeks, meals, lodging, and most expensive, the chemo treatments and medications. We have 40% co-pay on medication, plus our $875 a month insurance premium. The financial burden was staggering. Insurance is a totally different animal when it comes to FDA approved drugs, clinical trials and cancer medications. I could not believe that it cost this much money to treat cancer. As soon as I was recovered from the brain surgery and was able to function again, Shelly and I had to make our plans for the future. We came up with our action plan: to sell our business, resign my positions on the local water board and homeowners' association, and to maintain as much as possible my work and membership with our church. Without the aid and support of the church, I am not sure if my attitude would have stayed as positive. We decided to have a positive attitude, to research any and all information about my type of cancer and to examine all available treatments. We also made a promise to each other to remain faithful and loving towards each other. You both must commit to face cancer. I often wanted to die, but my wife would reach over and say, you can't die, I need you too much. I would switch from that frame of mind to knowing that my wife loved and needed me and I had to beat this cancer to be with her and to live the life we wanted. As the weeks went on and my parents were able to leave, I knew that Shelly would have to be able to take on some of my responsibilities. She needed to know everything from changing the air-conditioning filters, doing lawn maintenance, to taking care of finances and investments. We also started talking about where all of the financial files are, the bill filing system and sharing passwords for our financial information. We both had to know everything as we didn't know how long we had but we continued to remain faithful and positive knowing that we would have some good days ahead.

Shelly's Story

This was a difficult time for me. Larry's parents were still here, they were worried and I felt so bad for them. The first night that Larry took the oral chemo medicine he was so sick that you could hear him all over the house. His mother and I both bolted for the bathroom to see if we could help him and I took one look at him and knew that this was something he was going to have to deal with and struggle to keep going. I got a wet cloth for his head and got him back into bed and just sat with him and held his hand. He was miserable. I felt helpless to help him but I also knew that I had love and comfort to offer him. Once again we said that we would lean on each other and keep our faith alive, as better days would be coming. I decided to put Larry on an immune system supplement. After some research I decided on a powdered type that I could make into a big chocolate milkshake every evening. He loves chocolate and I knew he would be happy to have the milkshake as a change from the Jell-O he was living on. He would struggle to show me how to clean the pool, start the lawnmower, he stayed on me about educating myself on stocks vs. bonds, on what to look at in the market, on how not to panic when it went up and down like a yo-yo and he assured me that I would be able to take care of our house and property should he die. I kept telling him that I didn't want to learn as I felt like if I already knew most of the things and how to do them, he would not be needed and he would just give up the fight. I went along with all the lessons but most of the time when Larry was showing me how to do things I was just praying to God to not take him now and to leave him here with me a bit longer as even if I knew how to do all of this I would be so heartbroken that I could not function. I am so grateful today that God answered my prayer.

LARRY'S TIP:

Get your house in order. Be a realist but approach everything with a positive attitude.

SHELLY'S TIP:

Know what is going on with all of your business, finances, children and home records.

COUPLE'S TIP:

Get together and talk about all of your finances. Cancer is going to cost you money. Most of the medications that you take for cancer are different from regular medications in insurance policies. Check your insurance policies, life insurance, living costs, your assets, and your debts. Decide what is important and what is not. Make a priority list as we did on what you are getting rid of and what you are keeping. It is up to you as a couple to decide on your course of action. Do what you think is best for the two of you. People will come out of the woodwork, everyone will have an opinion on what you should or should not do, what you should eat, what cancer diet will kill the cancer, etc. Do the research, talk to your doctors and make the best decision for you as a couple. Trying to please other people with their remedies just puts more stress on you both. Just respond by saying something like, "I appreciate the information and please feel free to share any information with me that you find but now we are on an immune program that we don't want to interrupt." Take the information and handle it how you see fit as a couple, together.

Chapter 4:
GETTING READY TO DIE

Larry's Story

Physical and personality changes have occurred. After the brain surgery the bed was my life. Since I did not eat much, going to the bathroom was still a problem. I needed help for over a week. Thank you family, Shelly, church members and neighbors for everything you have done to help me in this battle against Cancer. All sense of modesty disappears but you want to hang onto your dignity. It is okay to tell people that you are not well enough to receive visitors. I think they want to show support and the last thing they want to do is stress or upset you by visiting when you are not up to it. I have found people to be very helpful when they realize that I need some help. They are kind and I think they feel better when they think they can do something to help you. People in your life feel helpless and don't know how to help you. Open communication with them is good as well. We would keep a list of things that needed to be done and when someone would call and ask if there was something they could do Shelly would get out the list and read the items off to see if there was something that they would be willing to do. We found people to be helpful and glad to run an errand or come and sit with me for a bit so that Shelly could go and pick up medications or do errands for me. After I recovered enough to move from the bed to my chair I was able to walk slowly and take myself to the bathroom. I would have to hold onto the walls or the edges of furniture, as I was very frail and unsteady on my feet. While I have recovered some strength, I am not able to return to my pre cancer physical abilities. I still get frustrated with myself when I can't remember names of things or forget something that I shouldn't or have written on the calendar. I remind myself how far I have come and remember that being positive is an important part of healing. I am feeling good but ever mindful of my next MRI.

Shelly's Story

The physical and personality changes were happening quickly. Larry didn't want to take a shower or comb his hair; he felt lousy and wanted to lie around. He would force himself to shower, brush his teeth and hair and get dressed. Even if he came and sat right back down in his chair afterward, he always got up and took care of himself. The personality issues kept me hopping until I adjusted to them. Larry would say sarcastic things out of the blue; he would be surly and just seemed to be looking to pick a fight. I would realize that he was undergoing changes in his brain. He would be okay one hour and not okay the next. He would follow me around everywhere I went like he could not stand for me to be out of his sight and I needed a few minutes to myself once in a while. I would talk to Larry and tell him that I needed some alone time every day. He tried to be respectful of my time and I tried to be available for him. We talked through these behaviors and it helped us to better understand each other's thought process and patterns. We have grown close because of all these heartfelt talks. When you are struggling as a person to keep your mind positive and get some time for yourself and someone is constantly following you and asking questions and demanding your undivided attention you expect to see a small child, when you see this in an adult body especially when it is your lover, your husband, that is a hard thing to get your mind around. It would be hard for me to keep my patience in check when Larry would come outside to get me because he couldn't find something in the pantry, I would come all the way in the house, move the bread or crackers and there would be what he was looking for it would drive me crazy.

Larry's Tip:

I thank Shelly and God that people put up with some of my childish actions. I felt that a priority was to act mature and be an adult. Shelly would coach me on situations when I was not behaving appropriately. Please understand that your partner with cancer isn't trying to be like this on purpose. Everything seems like it spins out of control and it is a constant fight to keep yourself together because you realize that this could kill you and no matter who you are, nobody is ever ready to die.

Shelly's Tip:

I would think, "Is he doing this on purpose to see how mad he can make me? To see how much I can stand before I blow a gasket?" and then I would take a step back and realize that, no, he did not intend to bother me he was just trying to relearn and readjust to life with a brain tumor. I had to give him a break, give me a break and talk to him about what he was doing that was getting to me. He would talk to me about his frustration level and we would work it out.

Couple's Tip:

When you are together all the time you do tend to get on each other's nerves. Normal life consists of getting up, going to work for 8 or 9 hours, returning home around dinner time, eating together and spending a few hours watching television before bedtime. Our life is NOT normal so we have to find a way to get along, be there for one another and have fun while we are doing everyday chores. The upside of cancer is it gives you time to think about what you want to be, what legacy you want to leave behind and the guts to do things you would not do in a normal life. Once again appreciate the time that you have been given and live life to the fullest.

Chapter 5:
THE MASK

Larry's Story

The first MRI after surgery was in May. Until now it had been nothing but the biopsy and surgery, followed by radiation treatments every day, the mask that they make for you when you get head radiation looks like something out of the middle ages that the swordfighters would wear. It was mesh and you could see through it. Knowing I had to put it on every day and they would screw it down to the x-ray machine so I could not move my head while receiving radiation was depressing. We would pass the time by talking to other patients in the waiting room; other patients are very informative and helpful in many ways. You find out you are not alone, the waiting room is filled with people with all sorts of cancer; prostate, lung, neck, throat, liver and you know that they are suffering right along with you. In fact I had lost all of my hair at this point and a woman who was there every day with her husband who had prostate cancer knitted me a cap. She saw me come in one day with my fuzzy hair and it was cold outside. A week later she presented me with a spiffy brown knitted cap that she had made for me. I wore it when I went to radiation and it felt good. We went on vacation in early May, as we knew that the first real test of how the radiation and chemotherapy were going would be in the results of the MRI. I was nervous about the MRI and just wanted to get it over with. The results were devastating; the last thing a cancer patient wants to hear: "The tumor has grown." Despite the surgery, 33 visits of radiation and Temodar chemotherapy treatments, the tumor had grown almost 28%! I felt defeated but realized at the same time that I had to focus on the positive and that there was another chemotherapy program or clinical trial that I could qualify for. When I got back home I started physical rehabilitation. I believe that lack of physical activity would result in poor health. Since I had not been keeping up on any of my chores due to the sickness and fatigue from the chemotherapy I started with the yard. At this point I had lost 50 pounds and still existed on green Jell-O. Be careful about physical exercise. If you work too much, you will take away energy that could be used to fight the cancer. Watch your health closely as you will have little to none in the way of an immune system. Many people will die of complications such as phenomena when they have cancer. Take an active role in your health, you need the strength.

Shelly's Story

The first MRI after surgery was a shock. I kept thinking that with the surgery, chemotherapy and radiation that the tumor would have shrunk. It was just the opposite. It had grown 28%! I just hugged Larry and said that we would try something else. There was a clinical trial known as CPT-11 that looked promising. We signed up, with many forms to fill out, and started Larry on CPT-11 through our oncologist, Dr. Andrews at Sacred Heart Hospital in Pensacola, Florida. We would have to go into the hospital as an outpatient every 21 days for chemotherapy. We decided at this point to have a port placed so that the chemotherapy could be delivered faster as Larry's veins were shot after the first four to six treatments. We waited too long to get the port put in. We should have done it as soon as Larry got stronger from the radiation. While at Moffitt this trip we met and talked to a wonderful couple, Julie and Bill Banquet. This was their first visit to Moffitt, and he had surgery and was there to start seeing the neuro oncologist at Moffitt. I showed her how to order the CDs of the MRI right there in the waiting room by the phone and they would give you as many copies as you wanted and you could pick them up after you saw the doctor. I told her about putting a book together to organize dates, doctor reports, MRI CDs and many more things that she would need to keep together. We would talk on the phone about our fears for our husbands; we would pray together and support one another. Her husband, Bill died; it was a very sad day. I broke down and cried, I cried for all of us, what a cruel thing to have happen to them. She had told me once that they believed that they could be the first ones to beat a Glioblastoma, grade IV tumor. They were positive and faithful as well. They did everything they could to keep Bill happy and alive. I miss talking to her, as now I am just a reminder of the tumor and the death and all the bad things that go along with those feelings. This was a challenging and trying time for Larry and me. We were so sad over the news that the tumor had grown but also very optimistic about the future and the new treatments within the clinical trials.

LARRY'S TIP:

Don't be depressed because of bad news. You have to gather your strength and emotions together at this shaky time and say, "I am not going to lose this battle."

SHELLY'S TIP:

Talk to people in the waiting rooms while you are waiting for your spouse. There are wonderful people in these waiting rooms and everyone is going through the same thing you are. You will find great comfort and good knowledge by talking with and sharing stories with other people fighting cancer.

COUPLE'S TIP:

When you receive bad news, as we did in the beginning, stop, don't panic. Realize that there are other options to explore. Realize that you have to put yourself together and be strong. Lean on each other. If you are angry, talk to your spouse about your anger, even if you want to say things like "How can you understand, you are not going through this!" Please remember that your spouse is indeed "going through this with you." They are doing the best they can to remain positive and absorb the news as well. Their entire way of life is on the line just as yours is. Talk, talk, talk, communicate with your spouse; don't shut them out and be angry. You are wasting valuable time with these emotions. It is all right to have them but you must move on to the positive thought process and pull out your faith; dust it off if need be. Realize that you are a fighter, you do not want to die, and that you will be a positive thinker for yourself and those around you. You want to be an inspiration to others, not a gloomy person that people run from when they see you coming. Think about it, whom would you rather be around?

Chapter 6:
FRIENDS AND OTHER PATIENTS

Larry's Story

Opinions, what we have learned from others; friends, co-workers and family members who have had cancer are all helpful. While some family members have had cancer, very few have survived more than a few months or up to a year and a half. However, with more and more people getting cancer and with the research that is being done, the odds of surviving cancer are starting to increase. I am walking proof that taking the medications, exploring your options, taking care to rest when you need to, removing as much stress from your life as possible, having faith and being positive, do work. I passed the mark when according to statistics I should have been dead and I am still alive, working, laughing, loving and enjoying my life. One of our long-term tax customers had breast cancer but after two years of fighting she was back to work and now two more years have passed and she now owns her own flower shop. A neighbor had a son diagnosed with a grade IV tumor while mine is a grade III. I met him and then I wrote him a letter of encouragement and suggested that he be a contributor to this book. He was having radiation as well as chemotherapy. He died 10 months after his diagnosis. I don't feel that he had the support, care or love that he needed. His parents were so far away and they went as often as they could, and to watch them have to go through this with their son was heartbreaking. I felt so bad for them and it just made me determined to fight harder and not become another statistic in the cancer arena. In summary of the individuals I know, attitude is critical. A person who chooses to give up, not take the medical advice or get involved in alternative treatments does not seem to last long. Shelly and I both feel strongly that continued research and continued questions to the doctors are important. If you feel that your doctor is treating you like a number or not taking the time you need to get your concerns and questions addressed, find another doctor! Don't hesitate to get other opinions; this is your life and your money that is on the line here. You have a right to feel that you are getting the best medical care available and it is up to you to make good choices for yourself.

Shelly's Story

Opinions; these came calling from everywhere. This was the best treatment, that was the best treatment and on and on. We took all the opinions, looked at them and decided what we wanted to do. Many people want to help and many people don't know what to say to you so they don't call or say anything. You will find that the friends that you thought were going to be there are not. The support and help often comes from people that were on the fringes of your life before cancer. When our neighbor stopped us on a walk last February to tell us that her son had been diagnosed with brain cancer as well, we knew her hopeless feelings. Our hearts went out to her, as we knew the determination and fight that she and her family would have to have in the months to come. When her son, a physician, died 10 months after diagnosis I was very scared wondering if Larry would be next. We have stayed in contact with the family. When you are involved in cancer and you see or hear of someone you know that dies with the same cancer it can make you very depressed. You have to realize that each person and situation is different and that you have to remain positive, helpful and get that faith out once again and talk to it. You feel bad, sad and mad about the fact that this young relatively healthy husband and father had to die but you also realize that it isn't you and that you have to keep on doing what you have been doing that works. These kinds of emotions can throw you to the bottom of hell's pit and it takes so much energy to get out that could be used for positive thoughts and direction. I have heard our preacher say over and over again, one thing is for sure, nobody is getting out of here alive but death is something that no one is prepared for when it comes.

LARRY'S TIP:

A recent publication listed 240 different cancers. Learn all you can about cancer, especially the kind you have. I put a priority on reading about and researching cancer. You must stay centered on your priorities. Also look for and read about new cancer studies. Shelly could find an average of 30 new studies every two weeks.

SHELLY'S TIP:

Don't let other opinions sway what you know is best for you. Don't be afraid that other people will be upset or angry if you don't use their methods. Trust yourselves and your decisions.

COUPLE'S TIP:

During this time of upheaval, uncertainty and fear you have to refocus your energy in a positive avenue. You have to practice Emotional Intelligence, the ability to motivate oneself, to persist in the face of frustrations, to regulate one's moods and keep distress from swamping the ability to think, to empathize and to HOPE! Don't doubt yourselves. Different things work for different people. We are all different, you know yourself, what works for you and what doesn't, find three things that work and pick one; try it to help you refocus your energy into positive action.

Chapter 7:
CHEMOTHERAPY

Larry's Story

As of this writing, there are two popular areas of interest that are being investigated for brain tumors. Many years ago polio was defeated by taking dead polio cells mixed with white blood cells and giving up to three shots with a serum made from polio cells. This alerted white cells to go after any polio cells. A similar program for cancer is being tried but the study declines individuals that cannot be operated on. Most studies are limited. Doctors seem to take studies one at a time. Another current study is giving patients venom from scorpions. There are questionable treatments available from Mexico and beyond. Chemotherapy kills the cancer cells but it also kills healthy cells. I strongly believe that to terminate cancer a medicine to kill cancer cells must be found. I realize that the best I can do is to remain stable, but the goal is to have a cure. I am thinking that the immune system will be the key. Currently I get chemotherapy once every 21 days. A typical day of chemotherapy for me goes like this: I go to the hospital lab for blood tests to make sure the red and white blood counts are within range. If they are not, I go back home and reschedule. If the blood counts are good then we go into a room on the chemotherapy floor, wait for the pharmacy to make and distribute the chemo, have a chemo-certified nurse to start administering the chemotherapy and lie in the bed and feel sick for four to six hours and hope that I can go home by 5 p.m. and just lie in the recliner and rest. The next five to seven days are crap. I don't have the energy to get up, all I want to do is sleep and I am not hungry at all. These are the times that I have to stay close to my faith and my wife. I have to remember positive things and get myself ready for next month. I tell myself that this chemotherapy is killing the cancer and I have to keep doing it, it is holding back the growth of the tumor and it is in the long run helping me live a longer life. I wonder about quality of life but know that these days will pass, I will feel better and I will survive this dreaded disease. I will not quit, I will not give up, and I will fight and keep living.

Shelly's Story

I would do constant research on the type of tumor that Larry had. I would go from website to website, checkout out the new trials, if Larry could qualify to meet the criteria, etc. Sometimes the more you research the more you find out that you don't want to know. If you get stressed doing this, stop, take it a bit at a time each day, and don't overwhelm yourself, as it is easy to do. Just trying to find something that would kill this tumor and these cancer cells was a full-time job. I would go to the hospital with Larry everyday for radiation and every 21 days for chemotherapy. It was always a long, grueling day. Sometimes things went smoothly and we could be in at eight and out by two but most times things went slowly. The pharmacy has to wait until you are checked in and in the bed before they would make and send up the chemotherapy. I always checked and double-checked what they were giving Larry as I always wanted to know what and how much and verify it was correct. Not that I didn't trust the nurses but I wanted to make sure I took an active part in knowing what Larry was receiving. Once his IV came out of the vein and started pumping chemotherapy into his arm. It was terrible looking, he had a big purple hard area that covered most of the underside of his forearm. I felt sorry for him. He had many bad days and would get impatient and I would try to distract him by reading to him, watching some mindless comedies on TV or talking about trips we would take in the future and what our plans would be and where we would go. I would talk about anything positive to keep his mind off the fact that he was miserable. Being the spouse and caretaker is a very hard job; you have to remove from your mind all of your selfish thoughts and agenda as this person that has cancer needs you more than you will ever know. They depend on your insight, comfort and love, imagine how you would feel if it were you. Remember the golden rule; do unto others as you would have them do unto you. Anger cannot be a part of you while you are helping your spouse battle cancer. It isn't easy, no one said it would be, but you can make it easier with your attitude. When you have a bad one it just saps energy from you. This is the fight of your life and you need to be ready.

LARRY'S TIP:

Chemotherapy is hard. I believe that this is where patients are apt to quit. If you want to live, DON'T QUIT! There are great anti nausea pills both IV and orally to help during the chemotherapy process. Life will get better, but this will test your strength and resolve, which only YOU can control.

SHELLY'S TIP:

Chemotherapy will be a hard time for both of you. Try to make it as pleasant as possible. Don't let yourself get overwhelmed, remember emotional intelligence, and don't let your emotions make you ineffective to your partner.

COUPLE'S TIP:

Larry was sick and fatigued quite a bit. If you like cards or board games or just talking to each other, now is the time to put these actions into play. You need to do extra special things for each other, get the ice cream cone, bake the cake they like, talk about your hopes and fears for the future. Bolster each other up, when one of you is down, the other should step up and try to make it as pleasant as possible. We realize that it is a terrible time, it hurts, it makes you sick and so tired but once again call upon your faith, and the positive attitude that you have built up. This is just another part of cancer trying to get you. You want to throw up your hands in disgust; this chemotherapy that faces you for many months is already defeating you physically and emotionally. Learn that your spirit and attitude are what will keep you going. The result of negative attitude during this time will make you feel even worse. Sometimes we as humans like to feel sorry for ourselves; we like to wallow in the self-pity and hatred of the cancer. You can hate the cancer, but don't hate yourself or your partner. Believe it or not, things could be worse, you could live in a country where no treatment is available or you could be dead. You are still alive and kicking and fighting. Don't quit!

Chapter 8:
RADIATION

Larry's Story

There is no pain in radiation. The specific area of the body is mapped via the MRI. This allows for equipment to only radiate the area that needs radiation. The radiation was every day, Monday through Friday. While there was no physical pain there was extreme mental anguish. The only information I really had was my scheduled times for radiation. If I asked any questions, I was referred to the doctor responsible in the radiation department. His only answer was "I can't say in your case; each person is unique." I was able to get some information from other patients. The position of the radiation department seemed to be: all of the patients are terminal, a few may survive but most don't. Having any relationship with the patient is not encouraged. The technicians that ran the MRI and who administered the radiation were personable but did not answer questions; you were always referred to the doctor, which was very frustrating to me. I believe the doctor and the staff were the worst example of a medical department that I have experienced. Each week I had an office visit with my doctor in radiology. We talked about amounts of other medications and my continued weight loss. One day while I was waiting for the doctor in radiology, he walked down the hall past me where I was waiting to see him at the nurse's station. He said, "How are you doing?" I answered "okay." He walked off and the nurse told me that I could go. The next week I received a bill for the doctor visit in the hall. I was enraged, not only due to his callous attitude toward the office visits with me but due to being billed for him saying hello in the hall. The next day when I went to radiation I walked over to the radiologist's office and walked in. He wanted to know what I wanted. I showed him the bill and asked did he recall that we had no office visit. The doctor replied, "I asked how you were in the hall and you said okay." I said that I had expected to see you in your office. I asked then for a credit for the office visit. He looked at me and said, "You obviously don't know how billing is done." I responded that I had a masters of science in accounting management, and it didn't add up to me. "Well," said the doctor, "we do things a little different here." The doctor explained that each patient in radiology has an individual program. It was estimated what the total cost of the planned treatment and was then divided by the number of sessions. The result is how much each patient is charged unless therapy is changed or ended. That said, I don't remember any other office visits. I resent that the doctor provided almost no information. I did not trust the chief doctor of radiology and still uneasy about the experience today. Shelly did not come into the radiation room with me but did verify medications and radiation dosage. The radiation techs made the experience tolerable; they were great guys with terrific senses of humor. I felt the doctor was a drag, due to his attitude toward me and, I would assume, his other patients.

Shelly's Story

Radiation was brutal for both of us. Larry was always so fatigued. He would get so upset because he had no strength or energy and we would talk about it and realize that he was doing okay. I think the worst part of this was that he lost his sense of taste. For a man who loves sweets, this was frustrating. Green Jell-O with mandarin oranges became his best friend. Before this I could never make good Jell-O, it would always be too runny or have hard spots in it. I became a pro at Jell-O. I could whip up a batch every morning in about three minutes. Even the smell of food could make Larry sick. We used to go to the Wednesday night suppers at our church but Larry could not even bear to smell the food. He would bolt for the door. We stopped going. I had to be careful of what I cooked and the smells it created or Larry would have to go into the bedroom while I cooked. Larry had beautiful black hair and when it started coming out in clumps he was very distressed. I finally told him to shave his head, that bald men were sexy and it would be minimum upkeep and he would not have to go through the depression and stress of his hair falling out every time he took a shower. I know he was sad to lose his hair. I was too but realized that the beautiful black hair did not mean anything in the perspective that he was doing something to battle and win over the cancer. I was proud of the way he handled the hair loss, this is devastating to anyone I would imagine. Questions like, will they still find me attractive? What will people think or how will they react? I would also guess that the person losing the hair would feel bad, depressed and unattractive. I feel it is the little things in life that push you over the edge sometimes, things like losing your hair and taste. These are indeed little things when you compare them to cancer and fighting for your way of life.

LARRY'S TIP:

Follow the doctor's directions no matter how much you may dislike the doctor. Don't sweat the small stuff. You will need to maintain your red and white blood counts or be denied treatment. I also know that hair can be an issue. Losing one's hair or ability to taste is better than losing your life.

SHELLY'S TIP:

The things that happen to your partner, mentally, physically and emotionally during treatment are challenging. Again, remember you are supporting and loving your partner during this grueling treatment. Radiation won't last more than six to eight weeks. The chemotherapy alone is better. Your partner will get stronger without the radiation every day. We would count the treatments left and that would make him feel like he was almost finished.

Think of things that you want to do together or something you want to accomplish that you have never had the time to do. There will be days that you are sick and tired and don't feel like doing anything, those are the days that you push yourself to do something positive, even if it is to make a phone call to a family member or a friend to tell them you are thinking of them. Start keeping a journal of how you feel so that when you are better you can go back and read it and know that you are fighting and getting better. Sometimes when we are at our lowest, reaching out to try to say or do something positive for someone else helps. It is okay to feel tired and sick physically, and to think about what you cannot do. What you can do is put your mind in a positive place, talk to each other, hug your spouse, write them a love letter, lie in the bed together and thank each other for being there. Think of things that you want to do ahead in your life because you know that your entire world and priorities have changed and you will look at things differently from now on.

Chapter 9:
COSTS

Larry's Story

Over a period of time my veins have gone flat and are very hard to tap. So like most patients I had a port implanted. A port is a rather simple device that is inserted in your chest right under the skin and is connected to a main vein. All of my blood work, chemotherapy, MRI contrasts and sticks are done through this port; it is much easier than getting stuck in your arm veins over and over. We have to go into the hospital as an outpatient to administer my chemotherapy due to the way our insurance policy pays. The insurance continues to climb yearly and the $875 a month premium puts a strain on the budget. Then you are paying 40% co pays on the medications so that drives our monthly insurance and medications well over the $3,500 mark. Can you imagine $3,500 plus a month because the FDA has not approved Temodar for use with brain cancer? They would pay for it to treat colon cancer but not brain cancer! I will be eligible for Medicare in 24 months. This is very frustrating as you are out of work five months before you get disability and 24 months before you have the opportunity to pick up decent insurance that is about half the cost of what we are paying now. The times when you need the cheap insurance and money to live on monthly are the times that you wait for the government allotted time to receive these much needed benefits. My wife and I talk about selling the house to have enough money to last us until I can get back to some kind of work. We don't want to sell this house as we have just remodeled it and love living here. It is peaceful and comforting in our home. We have carefully reviewed what we believe will be our financial needs. We plan to continue my immune supplement therapy. At this point I am on 33 pills a day. It is horrible to try to take this many pills in a day along with the chemotherapy and radiation but I continue to do so as I want to continue to be positive and fight for my life. I am worth it.

Shelly's Story

I continue to watch Larry suffer through the radiation and chemotherapy treatments. He is a brave man; he never complains but does get restless if he thinks something is taking too long. I watch him take these pills every day and choke and hack on them and he is just a blob in the chair most of the time. He tells me that he just feels so tired and sick all the time. I feel that he has so much medication that he is taking that it is just snowing him. I take all the pills to the doctor and go over them with him one by one, I ask what they are for and does Larry really need to take them. We reduced the intake of pills from 33 to 6 per day and that sure made Larry's life easier. He seemed to come back to himself more without all of the medications running through his body on top of radiation and chemotherapy. I wonder if I were in his shoes if I could cope with all the doctors and treatments and realize that my husband is a very strong, faithful, loving person who wants to keep up the fight so that we can do all the things we had planned when we married. Larry and I were only married a year when they found the tumor so most of our married life (we are now married almost five years at this writing) has been dealing with this beast they call cancer. I am proud and happy for us as no matter how hard it gets, we always hug each other, tell each other we love each other daily and always make a few minutes for talking together about where our heads are. I marvel at Larry's strength and also know that it comes from a faith stronger than him and from a positive attitude that no matter what happens; remains there.

LARRY'S TIP:

Pay attention to the details; know what each pill that you take is for. Manage your health along with the doctor; any new problems should be shared with your doctor, no matter how small. He cannot manage your health if he doesn't know what is happening. Manage yourself. Don't quit!

SHELLY'S TIP:

You fell in love with your spouse; you promised to love them in sickness and health. Sickness is a tough situation but love and faith and a positive attitude will get you through each day. Put yourself in the sick person's shoes, imagine what you would want someone to do to help you if you had cancer.

COUPLE'S TIP:

Remember your vows, and why you fell in love and the time you have spent building a life together. Love one another; continue to openly communicate with each other, we mean talk about it all. It is okay for everyone to have emotions, anger, sorrow and depression over the entire situation that you find yourselves in but this is what you have to deal with so deal with it. Once again find something to do together when your spouse feels like it, if not find a good comedy to watch together or just write how you feel in a journal. Your positive attitude will get you through the radiation days. You can do it, we did. We are no different than any other average American couple. Don't quit fighting!

Chapter 10:
REWIRING THE BRAIN

Larry's Story

Operations on the brain are a delicate procedure. In most cases it has been my experience that critical loss of ability and function do occur. Sometimes, total loss of sight and ability to speak or move can happen during brain surgery. The likelihood of getting back a function that is lost is uncertain at best. There are times, however that I feel the brain can rewire itself. Once a doctor held up his forefinger and thumb about a quarter inch apart and said, as much as we know about the brain and its functions, this is about how much knowledge we have. I believe that I had such a brain rewiring experience. I woke up early one morning before it was light, around 5 a.m.; it was Easter Sunday following my brain surgery in December of the following year. When I woke, I was not sure where I was but then knew I was at home in bed. I could not remember what day or month it was nor remember anything about what I was doing; I did remember that I had cancer. I woke my wife to try to tell her I felt something was wrong but could not speak. She looked at me and I just looked at her. She started trying to talk to me but I could not respond. We decided that I would just lie back and close my eyes and go to sleep, I felt as if my brain was rewiring itself! When I woke a few hours later, I could speak and went on to have a normal day. I knew the day and month. It blows my mind to think about how I knew that something was going on in my brain but was unable to get my mouth to respond. Looking back I am so thankful and feel extremely blessed that my brain was able to do this as I felt immense relief that my brain was recovering from the surgery. Other functional changes are memory loss. When I was an area manager for a computer manufacturer I would often forget to bring home the items that my wife would request milk, bread, etc. I would also forget first names after one meeting. I actually went to the doctor about this and he explained that your mind was like a blackboard and when you were managing things like $4 million dollar budgets, travel arrangements and employees that you would forget minor details like milk and bread. They were minor to me but not to my wife. The doctor assured me that I was fine but sometimes I wonder if this tumor had started growing way back then. Now I write myself notes to remind me of the calls I have to make, the appointments I need to keep and the important things I am doing in my life. It makes me feel as if I have some control and helps with my attitude.

Shelly's Story

I was so thankful that they brought me the papers to sign for consent for Larry's brain surgery; I am so glad that he didn't have to see them. They terrified me. They described the surgery and the things that could go wrong: death, hemorrhage, seizures, coma, and paralysis; it made my stomach drop to have to think about all of the horrible things that could result from the surgery. I wondered if the surgery to open his head and cut in his brain would cause side effects, how many and how bad. I signed the papers and just said "God if you need him, I will try to understand, I won't like it but please if you can let this go as smoothly as possible and help bring my Larry back." I was so relieved when he did so well. No problems, the doctor said. Once again I exhaled; I am getting very good at holding my breath and all my emotions in check during stressful and critical times. It has actually helped me grow as a person and for that I am grateful. One morning about three months after the surgery, Larry woke me up shaking me, I turned on the light and looked at him and instantly knew that something wasn't right. He could not speak and he just kept rubbing his head and looking at me. We decided he needed to go back to sleep and not stress about it for now. He went back to sleep and when he awoke a few hours later, it was amazing, he shared with me as best he could about what had happened to him and I could not believe how he was back to himself. I knew that Larry was going to fight hard and do everything he could to live as he felt like this experience was a lesson for him to learn that you can rewire, you can survive and you don't have to be so frightened of your brain and what it is doing. This experience in my opinion carried Larry a long way and he has talked about it since it happened; it was a significant emotional event for us.

LARRY'S TIP:

The brain is more flexible than we think. It can compensate for many problems. But the brain has limits, and your body will not return to your normal strength. The trick here is to realize that and continue to focus on the positive facts that you can still take care of yourself, you can still live life but at a slower pace for your body. You have put it through much trauma with the chemotherapy and radiation. A positive attitude about small steps fits well here.

SHELLY'S TIP:

When your spouse is scared, frightened or unsure, now is the time to comfort and support your spouse. Focus on helping them to feel calm. Nothing can be more frightening that wishing to communicate and not being able to. Don't panic or over react, remain calm and stay with them until they go back to sleep. Imagine if it were you. I wished I could have thought to give Larry paper and pen? I don't think he could have formed the letters; he was lost in his own mind. The side effects can be scary but they pass. Stick close to your spouse and your faith during these times.

COUPLE'S TIP:

As we have stated in other tips, attitude got us through this one. Larry realized that whatever was happening to him was beyond his control and to rest. I was able to comfort him and wait to see what he would be like when he awoke again. Comfort and just being there is sometimes the most important thing that you can do for each other. It is not a normal life, make the best of what you have and be grateful that you are both still alive and together. These are the times that you have to be thankful for what you do have (each other and quality of life) instead of what you don't have. This can be a hard one but the more you practice being thankful for what you do have the stronger you become.

Chapter 11:
THANK YOU JOHN HEWITT

Larry's Story

It has now been one year and three months since I was diagnosed with the brain tumor. I have had maximum radiation and am now on a different chemotherapy. As soon as I had recovered somewhat from the surgery, we sold our tax and accounting business, many thanks to John Hewitt for his instrumental help in selling our franchise. This was something new for us. We had been going through grueling days: taking chemotherapy and going to radiation every day and then to work until 9 p.m. We decided to make a good life for ourselves and continue forward in a faithful and positive manner. We went on a much needed vacation to Hawaii; we rode in fast boats and had a great time. It felt so good to have the sun shine on me, as I still got cold really easy. I remember we went on a snorkel cruise and the water was beautiful but chilly, I could only stay in a short time because I got too cold. I knew to keep myself in check and not do something stupid like snorkel when you are freezing and then get out into the wind. I did not get angry because I could not stay as long as I wanted. I was thankful that I could see this beautiful water and watch my wife snorkel. I could be thankful that I had a cancer and could go snorkeling. Once again be thankful for what you do have instead of what you don't have. Shelly had a great time and I enjoyed sitting in the sun watching her, I could pretend that I was doing shark patrol as hey, I had a brain tumor and nothing to lose I could save her if need be. Our sense of humor during all this is also a valuable tool. Everyone has a sense of humor, some more than others. Believe it or not, you will be able to grow your sense of humor greatly during these trying times. That is if you have a positive attitude, if not, then it will be a long, depressing, sad time. I have to ask myself, would I rather be spending some time with my wife, family and friends or would I rather stay at home and be depressed and upset because I have a cancer. Hmm, seems like a no brainer to me. We also started going to see our parents, grandchildren and friends. We soon discovered that we were living the life that everyone wants to have, free time, retirement, and not a lot of stress, unless of course you count my pesky brain tumor. We are taking walks together and talking and laughing. I love my wife.

Shelly's Story

During this time, Larry was feeling better, and he wanted to take me on a vacation. I said Hawaii would be nice. He said, "Then Hawaii it is." I never thought I would go somewhere like Hawaii. We all dream of taking exotic vacations but we were working and trying to manage a business, cancer and the house. Larry still was easily fatigued; he still is as of this writing. He would get frustrated about not being able to have the stamina that he once had, I told him that he was getting older and that the chemotherapy and radiation had taken a large toll on his strength. I said "Honey, it's your strength, not your life, we can get some of it back, focus on the positive you are still alive and able to get out and do things and go on vacation, while you are weak a lot of the time you are still living life to the fullest." We decided to start walking our standard two miles again. Larry and I both love sweets so instead of eating sweets and sitting in front of the television, we decided to walk and find some projects around the house to do that were on the "honey do" list but never actually got done. We all have those lists, the tasks you want to do but never have the time or money to do. This was a wonderful time for us. We didn't have the pressure of the business on us, we had gotten through the one-year mark and believe me it was a relief to cross that date especially since our neighbor's son who also had a brain tumor had died at 10 months. I will always remember looking back at Larry in that zodiac boat with his bald head and the wind flying in our face. I will always remember looking at him and living a truly content with life moment.

LARRY'S TIP:

I very much wanted to take Shelly to places she had never been. We went to Hawaii and had a great time. Sometimes I wondered if I was seeing these things for the last time but then I focused on the fact that I was here now and lucky to see it with the one I love. Make sure to enjoy this time, focus on the next trip you want to go on with your spouse, start planning, even if it will be a year or two. Dreaming is fun; we should all do more of it. Remember to smile in your pictures.

SHELLY'S TIP:

Know that as you go and do things, all holidays become bittersweet for your spouse. Christmas, birthdays, even the 4th of July. Tell your spouse how lucky you feel to be having this time with them, be extra positive if you can. I imagine that you would think of holidays and wonder if you would see another one. Put yourself in their shoes, stay close to them and remember to smile in your pictures.

COUPLE'S TIP:

Enjoy your times when you travel. Take more pictures and smile. Life is about living. Sometimes we get so wrapped up in the day-to-day grind that somehow we lose focus on the importance of laughing and having a good time. We shared hugs in the kitchen for no reason; A glass of tea together in the late afternoon before dinner to talk about the day. We often think that Larry could have died before or during the surgery. We realize that we have been given this time together and we are doing everything we can to enjoy it. Get a recording of your loved ones voice on the telephone answering machine or make some home videos, these will be valuable in the years to come. We have learned about each other as people, as friends and working together has given us another bond.

Chapter 12:
SHORT TERM MEMORY ISSUES

Larry's Story

Scheduling, paying bills and managing the household continue. With my inability to remember, I now make it a practice to make sure and write all events on the calendar. Paying attention to detail is needed. It makes you use your brain and keep it going. Don't sit around feeling sorry for yourself and being depressed; that does not help your brain. A gymnast has to work hard to keep their body in shape and you with a brain tumor need to remember that you have to keep your brain focused on the positive, the future and what you are going to do to keep things in order so that you feel that you have some kind of control in your future. My short-term memory is shot; I do things like come into the house holding the mail in my hand and ask my wife have we gotten the mail yet? Those times make you feel really stupid and inadequate but, hey, you were able to walk to the mailbox and get the mail. You are still able to stay in control of your home and finances; your spouse will help you. Shelly was always glad to help me. Sometimes I wanted things done and I wanted them done immediately, but she was always very good at stopping the presses and saying "Larry, I am not your servant girl to do your bidding" and I would realize that she was right. I, in my frustration, had started demanding her time and efforts when I wanted them, not when it was convenient for her. We have to work together as a team and sometimes my impatience was hard for her to manage and when she would point it out to me I would realize that I needed to focus on not being so impatient, being thankful that I have such a supporting spouse and grateful that I am here to grouse about it. We have to have these talks from time to time, as this is a two-way relationship. Doing things together makes me feel like a part of the relationship. Allowing your spouse who is also your caregiver to do all of the work is not fair. It is nice to be waited on but showing abilities to take care of yourself and do things for your caregiver is also good. Getting out of bed to help with cleaning, cooking or other household chores is appreciated by your spouse given they have assumed most of the responsibility during this time. Shelly keeps my medications in order as well as the other things that she has to look out for. She puts the seven-day pillbox on top of the dresser and fills it up for me so if it is in the box I take it. I try to keep up with them but it is something that she has done from the start and I don't feel comfortable doing it myself at this point. If you don't like the way certain medications make you feel, talk to the doctor about it; don't just quit taking them. I always appreciate Shelly for taking care of me and monitoring my medications and for putting up with my sometimes impatient and demanding ways. I realize that my brain isn't working right and I am becoming dependent on hers. I do, in my defense try to get her fresh flowers at least every two weeks. I always like to see the look on her face when I bring them to her. That is one of the things that life is all about.

Shelly's Story

Boy this was a tough one for me; I was trying to keep up with everything, the Jell-O making, the dog, keeping the house cleaned and making sure that Larry was comfortable. One night I was getting into the bed and Larry said to me "Shelly, are you going to get ice cream?" I replied, "No, I am going to bed." He then, I kid you not, whined like a 7-year old kid and said "I thought while you were getting your ice cream you could make my milkshake, I haven't had my milkshake today." My mouth hung open, are you kidding me, I thought. I said, "Larry if you have the mentality to realize that if I got ice cream you could slough your shake making off on me and had the energy to whine like that, then you can go make your own shake." He got up, made his shake and said, "Shelly, sorry I did that." I said, "Its okay, but it won't ever work." We had a great laugh and that is one of those things that life is all about. I would feel so guilty because I was doing everything I could, trying to make sure things were stress free and Larry would demand just one more thing and I would want to smack him! I told him it would be okay. I hugged him and said any man who brings me fresh flowers and makes me laugh can't be all that bad so stick around for a while and maybe we should have a glass of wine on the deck.

Larry's Tip:

Sometimes you need to talk to yourself and your spouse or caregiver about whether to fight the cancer or allow yourself to die. These thoughts weigh heavily when you have a disease that seems insurmountable. Keep communications open, you will need each other. Talk, laugh and realize that someone loves you enough to take you good, bad or ugly. I did not want to take advantage of my partner, but you need to be aware that you can become whiny, demanding and that is not fair.

Shelly's Tip:

I would think to myself, "Shelly what kind of Christian are you wanting to smack your spouse who has cancer?" Oh the guilt, but I finally realized that I am human and that my emotions need to be soothed as well. When I would feel like this I would talk to Larry and he would listen and then say whether he agreed or disagreed with me. Most of the time he would "say you are right, I don't know why I get so impatient and demanding, maybe I am worried about running out of time before I die." Realize that it is alright to get mad or aggravated at your sick spouse, you have feelings and you are an important part of the couple. Bring it to your spouse's attention if you feel that he/she is becoming demanding and dependent. They might get angry but it will also make them think of someone else besides themselves and the cancer.

You hear that saying that "In the long run it will all work out okay." You think, long run! It is the short sprint that we are doing now that we are worried about; the long run seems like a piece of cake. Our faith, love and respect for one another, our families, friends, church and our positive "Never say quit!" attitude helped us work through some of these issues. Every couple has issues but sometimes they are even more complicated due to a traumatic situation. You just can't take yourself so seriously. Everyone has bad days. As that old saying goes," it takes the bad days to make you really appreciate the good ones." When people call and whine about little things we just laugh, they will say things like "you just don't know how bad a day I had" and we laugh because if they want to compare bad days, we can sure tell them about those. One thing we have learned though this is that we want to put out positive and inspirational examples to everyone we meet. We don't want to be different; we're not. When you are relaxed and joking, having drinks and visits with family and friends they are much more comfortable and want to be a part of your positive attitude, nobody wants to talk to someone who gripes or complains all the time. We want to have people in our lives. We love our families and friends, they are so good to us, they love us and we get together and cook out and that is one of those things that life is all about.

Chapter 13:
FINANCIAL ISSUES

Larry's Story

My reasoning and ability to read and write has changed very little. Besides writing down things to remember, I can keep up with other issues by starting a file folder. I go back to the simplest things because it doesn't stress me as much. Currently I try hard to remember the things I need to. Shelly and I work on this together and discuss how to solve needed problems. For example: We make use of a larger calendar and write down all appointments. With the dramatic increase in doctor appointments, we now write down everything. We keep all the bills on my desk in a stackable bin and I can keep a daily check on the bill situation. This was very important to me because as an accountant I had always maintained budgets, stock and the checkbooks. Shelly was welcome to look at anything but I took pride in the fact that I was struggling back and becoming able to manage my financial affairs again with confidence. It was unacceptable to me to not be able to manage my own checkbook. When you have cancer it is a bummer, period. I don't care who you are or what you do, rich or poor, famous or not, it will completely change your perspective on life. I don't care what type of cancer it is, the fight must go on, you have to be positive, you can't dwell on what you can't do or don't have, you have to dwell on the future and how you are going to harness your positive energy and do something to help your mental as well as physical health. My attitude could be poor during this time, chemotherapy was nothing short of hell and my temper was short. Sometimes I don't react the way I should and I am slower. When these feeling get to me I realize that I need to lay down and take a 30-minute nap, it will help me with the fatigue which makes me nuts because I want to be up doing things and I am unable. The rest of the day goes better if I do this; I hate the naps but am learning that it is a small price to pay for what my body has been through. We try hard to support each other. We make adjustments in behavior when we feel we need too and try to keep a peaceful, stress free environment as much as possible. When I started bouncing checks and not remembering what checks I wrote or who they were to, I felt devastated. Instead of being down about it I decided to channel that negative energy into trying to make my brain faster. I felt worthless but tried doing simple math in my head and calculating my gas mileage and other mental exercises. After a couple of months, my brain was able to complete the task of keeping a checkbook.

Shelly's Story

When Larry lost the ability to balance the checkbook he was devastated. He took it so hard. He would say over and over, "I can't believe I can't even keep the checkbook!" I would try to reassure him that he would get better as time went on. The radiation had ended and the chemo was still going on. He started doing math exercises in his head, keeping up with the gas mileage on paper, anything he could add, he would. I took care of the checkbook and bills during this time and I kept telling Larry that I would be glad when he could take it back. I knew it made him feel bad and I really hated that because I knew he already felt bad from the chemotherapy. During this time of chemotherapy he would just lie in the bed when he was getting it and just constantly shift around. He could not get comfortable, it hurt his arms and he knew that all that poison was going into his body killing everything in sight and he knew how sick and tired he would be for the next several days. Month after month this man endured this treatment to fight something that he had a 2% chance of surviving and he beat himself up over the checkbook! I pointed out to him how well he was handling everything and that he should be proud of himself as I felt he was an inspiration to me. I don't think that I could manage through what I watched him go through as well as he did. He is truly grace under fire.

LARRY'S TIP:

When I could not add or subtract, I felt that my ability was zero. Without Shelly and her support I don't know what I would have done, thank you Shelly for your patience. Shelly helped keep me sane. Do mental addition and subtraction, try to remember things that you were good at and that you liked and practice that type of activity. Keep up with the gas mileage; keep up with statistics that interest you.

SHELLY'S TIP:

Watch and learn from your spouse, realize that the pain and suffering they are going through is a tough battle for anyone. When they snap because they feel so hopeless, tell them that you are there for them and put away your defenses. Anger, hurt, pain, hopelessness: these are what your spouse is living at this time. We will all need help in our lifetime at some point. We will need someone to love, support and comfort us. Remember, we all get a turn on the mat. Help them when they want to try to do something to get better. If they love the outdoors, put up a birdfeeder, and you will be amazed at the beautiful birds that will come and feed. I never realized until writing this book how much my support, patience and kindness and most of all love meant to Larry. I am a knitter. I wonder though how frustrated I would be if I had known how to knit for years and then forgot how to do it. Help your spouse practice. I never knew that I could keep him sane, I just wanted to love him and live as happy as we could in the face of the cancer. Try to help them through this very frustrating, painful time.

Together we decided that we would not yell about frustrations. The urge to yell and get angry is right under the surface but you have to channel those feelings into something positive and helpful. It is hard but is like being thankful for what you do have and not what you don't have; the more you practice talking things through calmly, the better you get at it. Learn to knit, take pictures, paint, Puzzles, find-a-word, online research, find something to do when you become frustrated and want to yell. The negative energy is no good for the stress level of your body. It makes your immune system even weaker and that is the very thing you are trying to build up. Don't destroy your good work over anger. Everyone gets angry but there is no use to yell at one another. You are in this fight together and you have come far. Celebrate your will and faith; celebrate your life. Appreciate it.

Chapter 14: LIABILITY

Larry's Story

Driving, I was upset about the driving situation. I was not allowed to drive. Can you believe that? I taught defensive driving courses at the college when Shelly and I met! I was pretty put out about not being able to drive. I resented it. I was a grown man and I could certainly drive. I wanted my independence and freedom but I also didn't want to kill other people because my pride would not let me follow doctor's orders. The doctor told me that he just didn't feel like it was safe for me to drive at this time because I had a minor focal seizure in December and you should be seizure free for six months before you drive again. This was a hard one for me so when I felt like driving I would get in my truck and drive up and down the driveway. It wasn't much but it did make me feel like I could get in the truck, crank it up and not lose the feeling of driving. That helped and the doctor told me that we would reevaluate my driving in May. As much as I wanted to drive, I knew that the doctor was right and in today's litigation happy society you never know what might happen. I started working on cutting the brush in the yard, I used a pair of clippers and just worked in the yard most days to keep myself busy, the weather was pleasant and I didn't want to sit around feeling sorry for myself. I turned to the chain saws; they were powerful and could get a lot of cutting done, manly man jobs! Who needs driving? I knew how to operate one, I thought Shelly worried too much about the chain saws but did not use them unless she was around after the day that I cut down a limb and it caught me on the fence and ladder and Shelly had to come and help me out. Shelly was most upset over the chain saws so I finally gave in and ordered one of those DR brush mowers; it is a fine piece of equipment. It is bright orange, black decals, cuts like an animal. This is a definite positive thing here in this brush mower. Sometimes being positive about things is tough. You are tired of being positive but you have to find some more gut and keep on fighting! Nothing like a big brush mower to help you fight!

Shelly's Story

The driving situation was very hard on both of us. Larry knew that he should not be driving but the urge to drive was stronger. He would want me to drive him five places a day, every day. I would comply most of the time but when he got impatient and demanding we had to sit down and have yet another talk about me not being his servant at his beck and call. I am his partner, his caregiver, his friend; I had a right to plans for my life. Sometimes the balance would be way off and it would have to be addressed. Communication is the key; you have to talk about things together no matter how mad or bad it makes you feel, being in it together is better than being alone. He broke the doctor's orders and drove to Lowe's about 2 miles from the house. When he came home I told him that he needed to think hard how important it was to drive as if he got into an accident and someone was hurt or killed he would have to live with the fact that his pride was bigger than his sense of responsibility. Not to mention the lawsuit we could face due to his neglect. He did not drive again until the doctor said that he felt safe for Larry to drive. Instead he turned to the chainsaws. I did not want to nag Larry. He would get the chainsaw out if I left home for an errand. Then he would write his mother and father and tell them all about using the chainsaw on a pole and his mother would call me scared out of her mind. I told her I wanted to break them all but knew that I would never get away with it. I would be aghast that he could even think of using a chain saw. The way I saw this was now I had two things to worry about, Larry with a chainsaw and Larry driving. I didn't know which one of these scenarios was worse so I tried to pay attention, when I would hear the chainsaw crank up I would go out and see what Larry was doing.

LARRY'S TIP:

I have pride. There is a difference between pride and doing something stupid. A car or truck accident could result in the loss of someone else's life or of all wealth including our house. Don't risk your future over a pride/vanity issue. You will get to drive again when the time comes. Patience is not my virtue but in this case my responsibility for others had to over rule my pride. I of course thought nothing of getting out the chain saws and cutting down pine trees. Find something else to do besides drive.

SHELLY'S TIP:

This is a hard one. It is my opinion and always will be that a man with a brain tumor does not need to run a chain saw. After the morning I fished him out of the fence and ladder, I asked Larry if he had a death wish with that chainsaw and suggested he buy one of those big brush mowers with four wheels that you push to cut trees up to 2" or something like that? He did and safety once again prevailed. Try to make your partner understand that his actions can harm others as his brain is not running on all cylinders and it takes time to heal. Don't complain because you have to drive them; just don't let them think you are their personal taxi available whenever they want. You have to manage your own responsibilities and priorities. Put your foot down if necessary.

Chapter 15:
HAVING FAITH

Larry's Story

This chapter is the result of talking to our pastor. We have great respect for him. His sermons seem to speak to us as a couple. We talk about the meaning of his sermons every Sunday on the way home or at night before we go to sleep. Shelly and the minister talked about when there is a crisis, people will stand and confront the crisis or fade and move on. We certainly noticed some friends and neighbors would stop by once and see what was going on or send a card and then we would never hear from that person again. During this time, I would hire people to do work I could not do myself. While the number of people that I hired for specific projects did not change, many people that I had not seen for some time came by to see if there was any work for hire they could do. I had to be careful, as it was my opinion that some were looking for easy money. But for everyone looking for easy money there were three or four people who just wanted to help with the fight. God bless the ones who want to stand and fight with you. Our families, friends that we ran with, our friends from the church and neighbors were so available to us and they all worked with us from their heart. It is a good feeling to know that people care enough to bring a meal, send a card, call and ask how you are. Some people fight and some people fly. We have been battling this tumor for about a year and a half now. While I am feeling good; each MRI is a test. I worry about our future. Shelly believes that each day is a blessing. While each day is not a fight, most individuals will drop out of painful medical programs. I know of a couple people who stopped taking the chemotherapy and passed on after a few months. While I don't know anyone firsthand, I have read about a number of people who stopped treatment and prayed to God about their disease and the disease disappeared. While I have faith, I admit that I would not stop a medical treatment in progress to rely on prayers or an immune system treatment. God helps those who help themselves. It is as simple as that. Taking an active role in your cancer is what you should do as a responsible person. Your character is being tested and that is something that nothing can take from you, not even life. The best way in my opinion is to follow the doctor's plan, talk to your doctor, have faith, remember that there are others who are much worse off than you are, have a good supporting spouse, have family and friends that want to help and to keep channeling the negative feelings into positive action. It has worked for me so far; I am halfway to my 36 month mark. I am still fighting and I will never quit!

Shelly's Story

We are a year and a half into cancer. The tumor seems to be stable and all is calm. Larry is feeling better, it is spring and it is beautiful outside. Spring just makes you happy. You are tired of being cold and the warm sunshine and flowers make you feel renewed. I know that Larry worries more than I do. One night I had a dream and I thought that God had come to me and told me "be at peace my child, the outcome will not be as they say." I awoke and thought boy I am really subconsciously struggling with Larry's cancer and the fact that it is terminal and he is going to die. I felt I had dreamed that because it was something I wanted so badly. I didn't say anything to Larry and went back to sleep. A week later I was wide awake and standing on the front porch by myself. All of a sudden this voice speaks to me out loud and says, "Be at peace my child, the outcome will not be as they say!" I almost snapped my neck jerking it around to look and see who had come up on me. No one was there and chills ran down my arms, I realized that God had taken time out to reassure me, not once because he knew I didn't get it the first time but twice, that the outcome was not going to be what they tell us. I don't tell many people this story, as they would look at you like they would if you told them you had seen a UFO. I truly appreciate my God taking the time to do this for me as it has helped me on many a day when I felt hopeless and scared that I was going to lose the man I had searched for all my life and had only got to spend three years with. I have always felt that God did that for me, as he knew the days ahead were going to be tough and I needed something big and safe to hold onto. I could not ask for more. After all when is the last time you heard anyone speak in biblical form, "Be at peace my child"? This is not everyday language. I knew in my heart this was my message to hold onto. What a great gift and it is still tucked in my pocket today.

LARRY'S TIP:

Individuals have power over you because you believe in the person. A coach can be a good person to talk to when you feel this way. Shelly and I found that our pastor was a good sounding board. If you don't have a pastor or don't want to do that then find a trusted friend you can talk to. Sometimes paranoia wants to come and stay but I have to keep him out, his brother doubt and their father fear is about more than I can handle so paranoia is not allowed here.

SHELLY'S TIP:

Whoever your god is, whatever you believe in, try to stay close to it. We believe in God and Jesus and that is what we try to build on. We want to have faith, not fear, we want to have hope, not despair. We want to have peace, not pain. We are just everyday normal people trying to build a happy, peaceful life together. You may see some signs of paranoia in your partner but talk to them and they will tell you how they are feeling. Resentment is something that can rear up as well on both sides. The cancer patient because they are sick and you are not, and on the caregiver side because you have lost the way of life that you were used to living, the mall, shopping, lunch with girlfriends, you can still do some of these things but you are much more restricted. Both of these feelings are normal you just have to confront and talk about them so they don't stew. Stay close to one another and enjoy this time when you are over the ugly, scary part and moving on to another chapter of cancer. Love your partner.

COUPLE'S TIP:

When your spouse comes to you with a dream or feelings, please listen to them. Your perception is your reality. Think about that one. How you perceive things is how you are going to react. Try to act and not react. Think about that one too. Celebrate the fact that you are still living a happy life together. Thank your family and friends for their help, prayers, effort and support. Keep up your physical activity, hobbies and traveling if you can. If you are lucky enough to get to go back to work, go; if not, find something or someone that needs help more than you do!

Chapter 16:
FINDING CLINICAL TRIALS

Larry's Story

There are many clinical trials and medical reports available online. We are always on the lookout for articles that our doctors have been involved in. I guess there are some reports that we consider more important. Since at this point I am receiving chemotherapy on a regular basis we closely watch my red blood count. I know that if it falls below four we can't have chemotherapy that cycle. That concerns me, as I don't want to miss any cycles; the sooner I get it over with the sooner I will feel better. Diet enters in here for us. We realize that sugar just seems to feed cancer so we are slowly switching the way we eat and drink. We are doing more drinks in the blender, mixing juices and supplements. I feel that it is important that I eat more eggs and more red meat at this time. My body craves these foods so I try to eat them, after suffering through losing my taste buds for six months and losing 50 pounds food tasted great again and I just had to have the meat. I have not missed any chemotherapy since I was diagnosed one and a half years ago. The next critical report is the MRI that we have every six weeks. That's right, every six weeks we have to go to Moffitt Cancer Center in Tampa, which is more than a seven-hour drive from our home, one way. We don't have a neuro oncologist in the Pensacola area so we have to travel for this care. Every six weeks it was a 1,200 mile round trip with the nervous anticipation on the way, the day of blood work, MRI and finally the doctor and the despair or relieved trip back home. It is a full three-day completely exhausting event. We are both very concerned about the size of the tumor, if there is progression (it is growing) or if it is stable. We make our list of questions to ask each time we go and review any changes that have happened with me in the six-week timeframe. Sometimes the doctor will have some information, but many times the doctor will not know the answer. Their standard answer is "It depends on the individual patient." We get quite a bit of information from other patients, much more in depth and real life experiences, more than the doctors. I have also found that experienced nurses can be helpful and comforting and very supportive. God bless these kind unselfish nurses. Cancer is like anything else in this world at times, if you have good medical insurance and doctors you will receive better care than if you are on Medicaid. Doctors don't like to take the state insurance. I am grateful that we can have the insurance and that I will soon be eligible for Medicare.

Shelly's Story

The clinical trials that are out there seem overwhelming. I made a good contact at Dana-Farber Cancer Center and Jeannie always called after every MRI to see how we were, and to email me any new studies or clinical trials that were available. Larry was beginning to eat everything in sight and I could not keep him full of eggs or red meat. I know that red meat is not good for you more than once or twice a week. Larry wanted red meat every day. I let him eat what he felt like eating because I had watched the loss of his taste buds and the weight loss. At one point the dietician was meeting with us to try to get more calories into Larry daily as he was losing weight so rapidly. He never complained; he was so happy to have anything that I made to eat and he just ate and ate. At this point he has started to put some weight back on, his hair is also coming back in as black as before and just as thick in the back and on the sides, the top is thinner especially where they did the radiation. He is vain about his hair and wants to have a full head of hair again. I tell him he will and he looks just as good as ever, I didn't marry him for his hair; I was just glad that he was functioning, laughing, doing things around the house and feeling good. I know he fretted quite a bit about the medical insurance and people that didn't have any or only Medicaid as he saw a woman and small child get turned away in one of the cancer doctor's waiting rooms as they didn't take Medicaid so the mother was informed that they could not help her. Larry felt very bad for this woman and he has talked about it several times since. He thought it was very unfair not to receive treatment because you didn't have the proper insurance coverage or money.

LARRY'S TIP:

If you don't get an answer, do research and reading on your own. Don't accept a zero response, or a vague response; work with other doctors on your team. Address issues to your managing doctor, the oncologist. You are not just a number; you are a cancer patient who needs answers. If they don't have them they should try to make you feel at ease with where your care is and how your health is maintaining. Bottom line, if your doctor does not know the answer to an important question that you have, ask who would know the answer.

SHELLY'S TIP:

Try to present food in a healthy manner for your spouse. Let them eat the things they crave during this time especially if they have lost their sense of smell or taste. Eating is near and dear to most of us so help your spouse eat properly. Also prepare the things they want, as this is a positive thing for them to be able to eat and not be sick. They have regained a small portion of themselves that was lost and this is huge for the recovery.

COUPLE'S TIP:

Go out to eat and have some nice dinners together if you can afford it. If not pack a picnic and go and eat outside somewhere. Know that maybe your spouse is eating too much of the wrong stuff but this is a short period of time and they are finally starting to feel decent again getting past the heavy duty chemotherapy and radiation. Continue to do your tumor research and keep yourself abreast of what is out there and possibly available to you.

Chapter 17:
TWO YEARS AND
TRAVELING

Larry's Story

We are now near the two year mark. The last several months have been quiet and laid back. We have done a few projects around the house and yard and are travelling a bit and working from home. We continue to do income taxes through our home based business. We try to keep a steady base of clients that we can help with their accounting and taxes. It allows us to earn money and have something to do that is positive and brain exercising. I feel that I am doing well, however I do make mistakes but Shelly always double-checks my taxes to make sure there are no mistakes or that I have forgotten to put something on the forms. We went on vacation to the Philippines with some friends of ours. We had a great time, spent three weeks there and actually found our way to an Old Catholic church in the middle of town for Easter Sunday services. While there my wife was receiving massages daily, the price for them was so much cheaper than in the States that it was a shame not to get them. One day she came in from her massage and said "Larry, the massage lady wants to massage your head." My response was no thanks. She came in the next day and said "Larry, she insists on touching your head." I agreed to try it to make my wife happy. I asked this girl about her training and experience in massage. She stated that she had been hurt in a serious accident and ended up in a coma for two weeks. When she woke she said that God had told her that even with her degree in accounting that she was to give massages and be a healer. She stated that it was amazing that she could actually feel diseases in people and I said yeah right, you already know what is wrong with me. Skeptical as usual, I like to call myself analytical. As she touched my head she said that I would not die as the doctors had said, I was not finished with my mission and I would be here until it was complete. Of course she didn't know what the mission was but I found it an interesting experience to be touched by a healer.

Shelly's Story:

Things remain quiet and peaceful. We have learned to live with the cancer. We all exist here on a volatile playing field. We talk a lot these days and I am pensive about the girl in the Philippines who actually said that Larry would not die as the doctors had said. Sometimes when you hear things like that you wonder. I never told her that the doctors had given him a specific time frame. It seemed like a reinforcement of God telling me to "be at peace my child, the outcome will not be as they say." This was a fun and amazing trip for us. The cultural differences and the people were very cool to get to know. Every morning we had a lady come by with fresh fruit in a basket on her head. She would bring fresh mangoes and pineapple and little sweet bananas. We were in heaven; we were steps from the sea and could watch the fishermen and divers. We felt lucky to have such a meaningful time together. One of those life time trips that you will always remember the colors and smells of the trip. When remembered you smile.

LARRY'S TIP:

Listen to people. You don't have to agree with the person but it does not hurt to listen. This applies to business as well as personal relationships. Everyone wants you to make it. You have been fighting for a while and they are inspired by your actions. Enjoy your life and don't quit. You are worth the fight.

SHELLY'S TIP:

Enjoy the calm quiet times. They may last a day or a month so enjoy when you can. Try to take some time for yourself. Treat yourself and celebrate the little victories in the battle with cancer. Ten years ago Larry would not have had a chance but now he does. Think about it, he has a 2% chance of survival. The odds are against him and once again my heart swells with pride at his attitude and willingness to help others. Tell your partner how proud you feel for them.

COUPLE TIP:

Celebrate the little victories. Pour yourselves a glass of champagne; toast your accomplishments thus far. You have learned that you can communicate, love each other, bend without breaking, you don't yell and let the depression get to you. You are learning to channel the negative into positive action. You are growing as a person.

Chapter 18:
THE TUMOR GROWS

Larry's Story

We were now at the two year mark; the appointment at Moffitt in May was disappointing. The result of the MRI showed that the tumor grew twenty eight percent during the past two and a half months. I have found that how you feel does not correspond to the size of the tumor. While I had been feeling better, not taking naps and feeling strongly that I was improving, I was not; the tumor had progressed (grown). My doctor says he is moving to Washington State; he has a better opportunity there. While I am glad for him I am sad for me and I feel uneasy as this has been my doctor for two years now, he has been the one to answer my questions, calm me when I needed it and watched out after my care. Who would the new doctor be? Would I like him, would I trust him as I did this doctor? It was a very hard visit overall, a growing brain tumor and losing the doctor that you trust all at the same time. I looked at Shelly and she just squeezed my hand and said "it will be all right, we have each other and this can be a good thing." Change is neutral, how you accept and respond to it is what makes it negative or positive. I decided that I would see what the new doctor was about and continue on my treatment plan. I have to start yet another new treatment as the CPT-11 Chemotherapy is no longer working. I have had 26 cycles of the CPT-11 and it has managed to keep the tumor at bay. I will be starting on a new clinical trial that involves a blocker that keeps the blood vessels from feeding the tumor to try to stop the growth. In theory it is going to cut off the blood supply that feeds the tumor and try to kill it. No food, no life. The side effects from this particular treatment are many but I feel that it is something I need to do to try to help myself. I am not going to come this far and then sit around and wait for a growing tumor to consume me. I am going to continue to go forward in a positive manner as I have learned to do and make a vow that I am going to do well on this program and finally find something to slow down or kill this tumor. Sometimes I think the chemotherapy and treatments are worse than the cancer. It is exhausting both mentally and emotionally as well as the havoc that it wreaks on your body. So many people give up because of the nausea and pain. There are so many secondary problems that come up associated with cancer. Somehow I have been able to get through it. When my odds to live are at 2% with the best chance at 15% I want to quit but know that I can make it, I don't want to be just a statistic, I want to shout to the world that I am going to beat this and I am going to share my experiences with others. The new treatment involves an oral pill but as I stated earlier the side effects can be pretty bad, it can affect your blood pressure, it can damage the heart. So off we go to start yet another program to kill the tumor, or worst case scenario, make me have a heart attack. I tell myself: Remember your patience, how hard you have worked to overcome the negative that constantly stalks you waiting to take your mind and run with it. Don't give up; be thankful that there is something else to try. It is promising and may actually help me. My doctor has moved on and I am a bit uncertain about the new one, he is so young, is he really a neuro man. Yes and I have to adjust to this change, he seems to care and wants to make me comfortable. I am feeling a bit hopeless and defeated but I know this too shall pass, every day can't be fun, there are days when you have to sit back and realize that you are stronger than this cancer and you will continue to fight and use the positive mental attitude that you are always building.

Shelly's Story

I felt lost after the Moffitt visit in May; we had come so far and now the tumor was progressing. We both knew that this meant the chemotherapy had quit working. Chemotherapy is a mixed thing, it is both a blessing and a curse, it can possibly cure and slow down the cancer and help you maintain yourself for a while longer or it can make you so sick and tired that you wished you were dead. I have seen Larry go through both of these emotions with chemotherapy treatments. I don't know about this new treatment, I feel that it is just too new to be using but also know that we were out of options. Larry said at this visit that he was through with chemotherapy and would try the new blood blocking therapy and immune therapy. Larry has said all along that the cure for cancer will be found in the immune system. He says it is the key that will unlock the information that is needed to defeat cancer. I know that for every few months that we can buy for Larry they are that much closer to some type of cure or treatment. I have reviewed 32 different clinical trials all over the country and do feel that the one the doctor is offering is indeed the best choice at this point.

LARRY'S TIP:

When I calculated a 2% statistic to live, I thought that the end was coming soon. I continued to live and decided that I would no longer calculate my odds of living with the new and untried experimental programs. My job was to live and be positive, not to sit around and wonder if I will be a statistic. I decided not to be a statistic as I had never been a follower or a lamb.

SHELLY'S TIP:

This was a trying time. Things had settled down and we were coasting and doing all right…only to be told that the tumor was growing. Don't panic; I can't say this enough. There are options and you have to let your spouse know that you are ready to explore every possible treatment. This is one of the times you have to help them to maintain a sense of control over the tumor. They realize that they may not have a chance but are ready to fight anyway; you make sure you have their back.

COUPLE'S TIP:

We were devastated to learn that the tumor had grown after remaining stable for so long. We were confused as Larry had looked and acted better in the past few weeks. We were stunned to hear this news. The doctor suggested we take some time to look at the new treatment. We did, discussed it, slept on it and decided that we would go forth and try it. We changed supplements at this time and went with an herbal tea mixture. We felt it was time to do some blood cell and T cell homework. We continue to make the decisions on what is best for us and it helps to take an active role in the fight. You have to stay in front of the eight ball, not behind it. In order to stay sharp, continue to read and educate yourself on your health, diet and attitude. In the face of bad news you have to gather yourself together and continue to support one another.

Chapter 19:
INJURY AND FORGIVENESS

Larry's Story

Now it is June. I am sleeping too much, tired much of each day and need a nap to be functional the rest of the day. I am tired, bone tired. We are trying to hang out with some friends and we go to help our friends with a yard sale. We take our dog Sam, and my wife steps on his foot while he is asleep and hurts him and he bites her fingers. Sam is mortified when he gets fully awake and realizes that he has bitten Shelly. I was angry with Sam and wanted to get rid of him. Shelly said no, he didn't mean to. I was not acknowledging Sam and he followed me around with his head hanging down for almost a week and I finally forgave him. I realized that I had to forgive the dog, as he did not mean to harm Shelly but to see her hurt and in the ER bleeding and in pain hurt my heart and made me angry with Sam. Sam has been with us for five years and he is a member of the family. We had worked with Boston Terrier Rescue over the past three years before I had gotten so sick we had to give it up. We fostered seven Boston's, helped find some of them new homes and transported some of them to south Florida when we went down to see my wife's daughter and the grandchildren. We got through this time with me learning that forgiveness is something you have to find in your heart. I am having trouble pronouncing words, words that I know, I am talking along and all of a sudden I can't find the word I need. I wrack my brain and still can't come up with it; it is like I am losing my mind and I know it. I have to really talk to my wife and myself as I am very frustrated by this inability to find words or remember the names of things or people I know very well. Shelly and I came up with a plan that if this happens she will supply me with the first letter in the word and that usually kicks my brain where it needs to go and I come up with the name or word. This helps me to exercise my brain as well. This is a stressful time for me; it seems like a long time since the surgery, radiation and chemotherapy have been administered. I am feeling so much better physically and wonder what is happening to me mentally?

Shelly's Story

We have been moving along very smoothly, yes the tumor has grown but the new chemo/biotherapy seems to be okay. It is still hard but we are adjusting to this way of life. I think the hardest thing about this is trying to make something normal out of something so abnormal. Larry has a master's degree and had begun to work on his doctorate; he was not a dumb man. He was brilliant; he often came across as eccentric sometimes because his mind worked so well especially in the math arena. To sit and watch him struggle with names of common items was very hard on me. He would get upset and we would just talk about the fact that his brain had been through so much in the past year or so and that he needed to not be so hard on himself and realize that his brain needed more time to regroup. I pointed out that his body was physically stronger and he was feeling better so just give his brain time to catch up. We decided that if he could not find the word I would give him the first letter, this worked well because he would remember the word most of the time, and every once in a while I might have to give him two letters but somehow the small hint always prompted his brain to get the word. This was a simple thing that we could do at home or in public. I would lower my voice in public so only he could hear we usually sat side by side when we were entertaining or going out with others so it wasn't so embarrassing for Larry. When Sam bit my finger it made me realize how much Larry depends on me. He was furious with that dog. The bite was my fault; Sam had lain down next to my chair and had stretched his paws out in front of my chair. I didn't realize it, and stepped down hard on his feet. He started screaming and I of course didn't think and bent down to try to comfort him and he was still half asleep and yelping in pain and he bit me. When he realized it was me a second later I actually saw the sadness and horror cross his face. I knew he was sorry and didn't mean to bite me. We both broke an important rule we always hear "Let sleeping dogs lie" and "Don't bite the hand that feeds you." I figured we were even. I got over the injury. It was very slow to heal and caused me pain but I learned from it.

LARRY'S TIP:

A pet can be a positive help when you are sick and in bed or a recliner chair a great deal of the time. Sam is a good dog and very smart. I am glad to have him for a companion. We all make mistakes, dogs included, and forgiveness is something that I want to be able to give. I don't have energy for anger and resentment. Those are negative and are counterproductive, you may want to carry them but they are worthless, lay them down and continue living and appreciating your life.

SHELLY'S TIP:

Crappy things continue to happen in your life: flat tires, dog bites, the faucet that leaks, the trash bag that breaks the every day responsibility that goes with life. You are not an exception because you live with cancer; cancer only magnifies these events. Sometimes I am grateful for the little things like seeing a beautiful blue sky or hearing the birds. This cancer has taught me to be a much calmer and more thankful person. I am grateful that Larry and I are still living, laughing and loving. Stop and think of all the things you do have, you're eyesight, your hearing, the sun on your skin, the smell of rain, how good your favorite foods taste, the smell of a baby. They are small but they are a part of life that you always hurry by, now is the time to look at these things.

COUPLE TIP:

Work together when you have a problem, the first letter word game worked great for Larry. He didn't have to suffer through the embarrassing public blunders or frustrate himself trying to find a word or name of something that eluded him. Be kind and respectful to each other. Be there for your spouse so they know they can depend on you to have their back and remember to be grateful and appreciative of the caregiver who is watching your back. Kindness is a good feeling. We should all practice more of it.

Chapter 20:
PHYSICAL ISSUES

Larry's Story

I began to have severe diarrhea all the time. I started taking Imodium with no change. We thought that it must be the biotherapy or supplements. Upon continued review, we decided that perhaps the supplement was the issue. After stopping use of the supplements the diarrhea was gone and now after three days, I was feeling more like myself again. This is a good topic to talk about with your spouse. While it sounds gross and is gross the fact of the matter is that accidents when the patient is not at home will happen. Clean underwear, towel, soap and outerwear may be needed. While my wife understands, many of the spouses of other cancer patients have not so understanding. We know of two couples with cancer that have fallen completely apart due to lack of communication, faith, respect for one another and kindness. This is why it is good to talk about what to do and how to handle it. You are both involved; you should both have a say in how to work things out. When I am sick and unable to function and someone drops by, even if they bring a gift or food, Shelly is always polite. She is good at conversing with neighbors and guests and lets them know in a non offensive way that I cannot be disturbed.

Shelly's Story

The diarrhea was sudden and severe. We would have plans to go to dinner with our friends and we would have to cancel at the last minute due to the bouts of diarrhea. These were tough times on Larry as he wanted to try to be as normal as possible but it was impossible with the runs every 10 minutes. The worst would be when we were out somewhere and he could not hold it. I would just deal with it and try to make light of it. After all, we all have these bodily functions and when you put loads of radiation and chemotherapy into your body, all bets are off. We talked about it and Larry was mortified that this was happening to him. I have two children and three grandchildren so dealing with this was not pleasant but something that I had seen before. I felt sorry for Larry, as I knew if this happened to me I might die of embarrassment. I am proud of the way Larry handles these types of situations. I think a man who can talk about these kinds of things to try to get me to help him or give him some ideas on what should he do was all that needed to be said. Larry is an inspiration to me in so many ways and when he puts our feelings on something like incontinence before his embarrassment, he is trying to make our lives easier.

LARRY'S TIP:

If a serious problem like this develops, talk to your partner about it or your caregiver. Talk to the doctor; check your supplements or pills to see if they are making you sick. Make sure you are thinking clearly about anything that may be bothering you. Walk through what is happening to you emotionally and physically and narrow it down because you know your body by now and you know what the problem might be if you don't panic.

SHELLY'S TIP:

When you marry or promise yourselves to one another the words are "in sickness and health", "for better or worse." Well guess what, you are now living in the sickness and worse parts. You hear these vows and think yeah yeah, I will always be there for them. Some people cannot handle the sickness and worse parts; they want the health and better part. You have to be the gatekeeper when your spouse is feeling bad with nausea and diarrhea and people want to visit. You want to make sure that you are there for your partner, who is going through these sick times; they need you to be there to protect and support them. The up side of this is you get to chat with people and get to know your spouse's friends as well as you know your own. Our friends all mix so well together and we have such great times with them. When you have friends that love and understand what you are going through they take the last minute cancellations in stride and ask what they can do for you. Those are the people you need in your life. Surround yourselves with positive, understanding people. Don't let negative people steal your joy or your time.

A rough sick time is hard to handle especially when you have been doing well for over a year. Yes the tumor has grown but you are still feeling better and the new biotherapy gives you hope. You have to tell yourself that you have another MRI in six weeks and that the new biotherapy has stopped the growth. You have to say out loud every day even if you think it is stupid that "We are winning this fight with cancer." Don't fret about something you can't do anything about. You were feeling fine and the growth occurred so you can't tell if it is growing or not at this point. It is like living with fire hanging over your head all the time and wondering when it is going to fall and burn you; the old saying is waiting for the other shoe to fall. Sometimes you just have to say, it will fall when the time comes, and move on forward with your plans. You walk with one shoe and make the best of the situation. Better days lie ahead and you have fought this thing almost two years now. Don't quit.

Chapter 21:
AFTER A TWENTY EIGHT PERCENT TUMOR GROWTH

Larry's Story

We are looking forward to a new MRI early in July. After the twenty eight percent tumor growth I am anxious as to what the MRI will show. I tell myself that I must remember to keep fighting; I can do nothing about the growth. We will know if the new clinical trial is working, the biotherapy; Sutent. So far results for this trial have been neutral at best. We will get numbers and status on patients when we see the doctor. If the results are anything but positive, then we will apply on an ongoing basis to get into an immune therapy program. We believe that this is the most likely cure for cancer. Doctors have not disagreed with the premise that immune therapy is a viable potential cure. I asked my doctor at Moffitt why he was not working with a highly potential cure like immune therapy and he said that the lab was not able to handle immune therapy work at this time. I understand that the FDA is a large part of why it takes so long to get a clinical trial from phase I to phase III and released to the general public. It seems to me with all the recall ads on drugs that they would relax the programs for cancer treatments. You have nothing to lose in trying new drugs as you already have terminal cancer. I, as a cancer patient would jump at the chance to try something that they were having great success in the labs with. It is risky but so is feeling sorry for your self, being upset and not wanting to help your self and do nothing. It takes on the average from 6-10 years for these trials to go through the phases and be deemed safe enough for cancer patients to take. We have been researching some vaccines available in Switzerland. If we end up going there it will be at our own expense. While we have limited cash, Shelly is strong and determined to do whatever we have to. I am going to keep fighting and staying positive. Hey, a trip to Switzerland may not be such a bad thing.

Shelly's Story

The time between MRIs, that short six weeks can be hard to live with when the cancer is growing. All kinds of things go through your head. You want to hope that the new therapy, this one, the biotherapy is going to kill or stop the tumor from growing but doubts want to creep in all the time. It is a fulltime job at this point to keep doubt at bay. During these times I have to go back to the voice on the porch and know that I was told twice that the outcome would not be as they said so I had to hold on to that. I was living on nothing but faith and I was not going to let it go. We were on our first cycle of the new Biotherapy and we could hardly wait for the MRI in July. Stay busy helping others and doing special things for your selves. Don't wish the time away, if the tumor is growing or stable remains to be seen and you can't do anything about the outcome.

LARRY'S TIP:

I want to go on record as saying that the cure for cancer will eventually be found in immune therapy, just like polio and smallpox. Utilizing your own immune cells out of your body carries the key. Your body made it; your body can kill it. Remind yourself that you are a fighter and temporary setbacks will not keep you down.

SHELLY'S TIP:

Doubt is all around me and I realize it is there but keep moving forward in my daily life with a positive attitude. Terrible thoughts run through my mind and I just can't face them. I don't feel like it is time to give up. Larry is making progress and he is still here with me. I just kept focused on the future and getting out and doing things, going on a picnic, sitting out back and drinking tea, having breakfast out on the deck and looking at the scenery all around. Enjoy your time together, do something positive. Talk about the next trip or vacation.

COUPLE'S TIP:

The cancer patient is trying not to live in fear. The ones that love them are trying not to live in fear. You think how crazy it is that you can control so many things in your life but you can't control what is happening in your brain. It is a helpless feeling, no matter what kind of cancer you have. Regroup, talk about your expectations for the next MRI, how you will handle good news or bad news. Enjoy each other and do simple things. Appreciate your surroundings. Appreciate your life. Ask your friends and relatives to stop by and visit, talk to them about your apprehension, people understand when others voice their fears, we all have them and people want to help you overcome your fears because it also helps them to overcome their fears, ask them to pray for you.

Chapter 22:
TERMINATING THE SUTENT BIOTHERAPY TRIAL

Larry's Story

We are on our way back to Moffitt. After the MRI the doctor informed us that the tumor had decreased in size over 25%. (Note that the last MRI had revealed a 28% growth). While I am thrilled with this news and it is always good news when a tumor does not change or decreases in size, the truth remains that chemotherapy does not kill cancer. We have received additional information on the gamma knife program in New York; there is a limit to how much cancer the gamma knife treatments will address. In my case, if it gets much larger, it will be too large for any gamma knife procedures. We will continue on this present clinical trial, the biotherapy called Sutent. As long as it is shrinking the cancer, we will stick with it. No matter how many programs I read and hear about and want to jump on I realize that I must remain with what is working. The old saying applies here: If it ain't broke, don't fix it. I was relieved for the decrease in the tumor size. Shelly and I had a long discussion about all of this on the way home from this visit. We discussed the gamma knife procedures, the immune therapy, the biotherapies, and chemotherapy; to at which time I decided there would be no more chemotherapy. I had gone the cycles through the various chemotherapies; the biotherapy, Sutent, seemed to stop the growth of the tumor. Again we wish that there were more powerful things that they could do involving the tumor, if only more drugs could get through the blood/brain barrier, that is I guess the big difference between brain cancer and other cancers, they are all bad and no one should have to deal with them, but when you radiate the brain it really affects the rest of your body. When you have cancer in your body, it doesn't affect your brain but when you have brain cancer your brain controls your entire body. Sutent decreased blood flow to the tumor, it also decreased blood to many parts of my body, and I was having severe cramps due to not enough blood circulation. The doctor agreed and I terminated the Sutent clinical trial. I feel that the Sutent biotherapy program would have killed me. I believe that I left the program in time to prevent permanent damage to my heart. It was a tough decision to make but I feel that we made the best decision for my health and I felt relieved to be out of the trial.

Shelly's Story

I was very happy to get the news of the decrease in the tumor size. I was still reserved in the news as during some of my research I had run across a blip somewhere that said often time the tumors shrink before they explode with growth. Since I saw that and believed it I would hold my breath until late August; it is now early July. I am not going to get worked up and I constantly tell myself to remember the voice on the porch, to stay positive and try to enjoy the summer. I was doing a lot of research for bio and immune therapy programs. I was reading about and hearing about all types of new trials and treatments but you can't go jumping from trial to trial. It is a difficult decision you have to make on which treatment you believe will help you the most. I so far have managed to let Larry pick his treatments and support his decisions. We have not disagreed on the treatment routine. I am starting to see things in this Sutent that I am not sure of. I notice that Larry is unsteady on his feet, has trouble rising from a chair without support and leg cramps almost every night. We talked with the doctor about discontinuing this program, as the downward spiral that we were seeing was very rapid. Larry had trouble getting up, walking, balancing, thinking, focusing on anything more than a few minutes and he began to pace around all the time. He could never be still, it was like something was boiling inside him and he just could not be still. We agreed that the cure was worse than the cancer and it was time to step up and stop it and know that we were doing the best thing for us and the quality of Larry's life. He could not handle this trial any longer. I was relieved with his decision to stop. I wanted to beg him to stop and when he would ask me what I thought I would have to be ever so careful in my answer as I didn't want to influence his decision on what he wanted to do for treatment. I would say "Larry, it is making you miserable, that is the only thing that can be making you feel this way as the only other medications that you are on you have been on for months with no reaction. I don't think this program is giving you the quality of life you want." He decided that he had to stop it or it was going to kill him.

LARRY'S TIP:

Open communication with Shelly and the doctor was critical. While we have stated the communication is important, the lack of good and timely communication would have resulted in death during the trial. It was time to act and I did so. Thoughts ran through my mind that I would now be without any chemotherapy or radiation since the tumor was diagnosed. Would it come back in record time? Did we have time to get into an immune therapy program? There were all sorts of questions running around in my mind. Stop Look and Listen. No need to panic. You must continue to fight and take an active role in your exercise, nutrition and mental state of mind.

SHELLY'S TIP:

Try to keep a focus on the trial that you are on. You and your partner have researched and decided what the best is for them at this time. You can't jump around clinical trials. That is like jumping around in the stock market. You want to because maybe there is something a little better out there, something that might kill the tumor. Don't. Just continue making the best decisions for your selves and try not to doubt yourself. Don't let doubt rob you of joy.

COUPLE'S TIP:

Take the good news and celebrate the little victories. You have to continue to celebrate yourself and your fight against cancer. You are surviving, you are living, you still have fun, eat well; enjoy your family and your friends. Keep doing what is working for you. There will be information overload and you need to realize that you are in control of which information you want to explore and which information you want to let go. You can never have too much knowledge but you do have to realize that you have researched and picked the therapy that you are currently on and that is what is best for you. Don't doubt yourself. We are doing well, we are happy. We are blessed and happy to see another autumn together.

Chapter 23:
THE DREAM

Larry's Story

Shortly after starting radiation and chemotherapy, I became aware of what a short time most people lived with brain tumors. The nausea, headaches and medication spelled a short continuation of life, even when there was a committed caregiver. Over 50% of people I actually had direct knowledge of quit the programs and trials with death following within a few months. This I just could not seem to grasp. I was being positive and never missing my medication or appointments or supplements. My greatest concern was that I would leave my wife, Shelly, so we talked about the situation a few times. She has many good years left, as she is 10 years younger than me. (I am currently 60 and she is 50.) I told her that she should find a new man, get married and continue life. She said that she had no intention of any more relationships. While she said this, common sense would suggest that she continue life and find another partner who isn't sick. I gave much thought to this issue. I thought much about what would happen to my Shelly after I was gone. The following dream occurred twice. The first time was in March and the second was in July.

The Dream: While sleeping, my tumor grew so large that it pushed my brain down and with the loss of oxygen my heart stopped. I was outside standing beside an oversized door to an old stucco three-story building. I knew that I was not to move around but to wait by the door. Within a couple of minutes the door opened and a middle aged white man in Biblical dress, blue striped robes to be exact, told me in English to come in. It was St. Peter. I asked where I was and he just looked at me. He then said that this was what I called heaven. He said that all individuals here were Methodist and that each religious sect had their own area; I wasn't sure about this but thought it might make sense. Moving into the center of a larger room, I realized that the walls and ceiling were all the same off white color, no doubt from age and lack of maintenance. The room was empty; void of furniture, the center of the room had a stairway up from this ground floor. There were also three metal poles that started on the third floor and stopped on the first floor. It reminded me of a firehouse where you could slide down a pole to the main floor. I followed my guide up to the second floor. There were 40-50 people on the floor. Upon looking around I noticed no gold walkways or streets. The people on the second floor ranged in age from teenagers to the very old but all could walk by themselves. Jesus was across the room looking at something written on one of the many tables in the room. Tables and benches with a few chairs took up over half of the floor space. My guide told me I would get a permanent location assignment during the day. We started for the stairs but a rush of people coming down the stairs and a few coming down the poles delayed us. I asked what was going on and he said that another person needed help. We then went to the stairway back to the first floor. About 10 to 12 people were looking over the balcony railing. A balcony went from the back made up of the same type of dull stucco. The floor was all concrete. No decorative touches. Looking down from the balcony a person was talking to another. A person near the rail paid full attention to the person below, a middle-aged woman. The 10 to 12 people joined the man looking down from the balcony. He was being comforted and all put their hands on his head, shoulder, back and on each other's shoulders and started to pray. I asked my guide what was happening. The reply was that the person on Earth had to make a decision and all were praying that she would make the right decision. The guide explained that there could be no direct communication with those on Earth but that the prayers directed to the woman on Earth would appeal to her conscious thought and moral beliefs to encourage a decision that was in her long term best interests. The guide explained that I would be able to watch over Shelly and that when I needed help, all I had to do was to pray and that people would arrive for support just like in the case of the man on the balcony looking down at the woman on Earth. My guide said that it was important to understand that the individuals on Earth were free to make any decision good or bad in accordance to the individual moral positions. Walking back into the center of the room we walked up the stairs to the meeting area with the tables. Jesus was getting ready to leave and saying that he had to go. We then walked up to the third floor. The building did not change the same off white concrete stucco. The third floor was more for prayer and meditation. The room was somewhat darker. Only natural light was observed. No artificial lights but the second floor and the first floor had more light. I did not notice any windows but there were open areas higher up on the walls. The guide excused himself but said he would return. After about 15 minutes I walked over to the stairs and went to the first floor as I looked down from the balcony I could not see Shelly directly as she was inside a large whitish building. She was not talking. Had she been talking I would be able to hear her. She came out of the building and I could see and hear her on the cell phone. Later the guide came back and was looking for me. He said he got my assignment while he was upstairs. I would be assigned this group. I felt good about this since Shelly would still be in my life. I know this probably leaves the reader with many questions like I have. Unless my guide was an angel I saw none. There were no areas for eating but there were baskets of fruit and people seemed to be eating the fruit. There were no food preparation areas. I also noticed no private areas or restroom facilities. No offices or medical facilities. But then I was not looking for everything. I was overwhelmed to be there. My mind was so much on not being separated from Shelly that I did not even think to look for my grandmother or grandfather whom I was named after. By being assigned I felt I had a new home but I recognized only one person in the group that I would be in. I had no idea if new people came in on a regular basis but the room was large enough to accommodate another 50 people. I had to have an answer to not having contact with Shelly. If Shelly would remarry would this change my ability to watch over her in the future? Also if Shelly would pass would she come to this location? I guess no one can predict what would happen but I wanted to know. This was a dream that I had twice; the first time I had this dream I was unsure if it was indeed a simple dream or a message. I have thought about the dream from time to time. I shared the dream with Shelly. The second time the same dream occurred I took it more seriously. I talked about the meaning with Shelly. I did not ask her then if she thought it was a message from heaven. I asked her later what she thought and she replied "It was a message for me." We talked about over her life that she had received a couple of messages which she described as a voice/ thought that she was to pay attention and act in accordance to what the message was. Shelly has more faith than I. I know that I should not have doubts but my personality is geared to facts and figures. I am an accountant and business owner with a definite analytical mind.

Shelly's Story

The dream was amazing to hear. I know that Larry is so afraid to leave me here alone. He loves me and I make him laugh and feel alive and he does the same for me. I always tell Larry that the God I know will not put us together for just a few short years, that he has big plans for us we just don't know what they are yet. I realized that Larry was subconsciously so full of fear at leaving me that he dreamed himself into a place that he could still be with me by watching over and listening to me and praying for me. That is true love and I am one lucky woman to have a man love me that much in my lifetime. When Larry started talking to me about finding someone else blah blah blah I just looked at him like he had three heads. I asked him was he nuts and I wanted some of what he was taking! He laughed and said "No Shelly, I am serious." I told him that I was not finished living my life with him yet and if he didn't mind could we see how far we could go together before he kicked the bucket. I told him he still owed me a vacation and I wanted some more things done around the house and it was wishful thinking to think he was going to die and get away from me that easily. Seriously, I told Larry that I was not going to discuss a future man that it was going to be hard for me to have anyone as I would always make comparisons to him and that would be so unfair. I would not want to put me nor anyone else through those emotions. I know that Larry and I will be together until it is time for one of us to pass on. Who knows, it could be me. Accidents and illness happen to lots of people. I just pray that God will keep us safe and together so that we can continue living the life that most people strive for and never have. After I told Larry that that there was no man walking that I would rather have and he should quit talking about it, he seemed relieved. He sure does hug me tight all the time. I love my husband.

LARRY'S TIP:

The dreams seemed real. I am not a person that has dreams. The dreams were an experience that I have not shared with many people. I guess that the dreams were the result of my constant thinking about Shelly and what would happen to her after I was gone. Try to realize that you have many worries and maybe a top three list. When you have dreams or significant signs, stop and think about them. Your sub conscious (the red flags) is a strong thing. Let it have a chance to come out and talk too. Everything in you needs to stay focused and calm and positive because just like in battle, you have to have a plan and you can't fall apart and expect a victory. You were always told if you panic you will drown, this applies at this time. Focus on your faith, future and living your life one day at a time. Be kind to yourself.

SHELLY'S TIP:

When Larry started talking to me about finding someone else, it broke my heart. I cannot imagine my life without him and can't imagine going through meeting someone again. Your partner is scared and they feel abnormal and out of place and step. Reassure them that they are who you want and love and make it clear up front that they are not going to leave you that easy. You are going to continue to fight this cancer together so that you can go on your next trip together. Doesn't matter where or when you go, doesn't matter how long you stay gone, you just want to keep something in mind to look forward to.

COUPLE'S TIP:

Continue to talk about your hopes and fears, your feelings of anger or disappointment or hope. Invite some of your friends over for dinner and talk about normal world events and what is happening in the political arena lately. Just talk to your friends about their lives and what everyone has going on. It is time to plan to have some fun. Celebrate with a mini trip for just the two of you.) Do something special together and appreciate your life and your health. Be grateful again for what you do have.

Chapter 24:
ONE DAY AT A TIME

Larry's Story

We are coming up on the late August MRI. I feel good but I have second thoughts, as my MRIs have not been stable. I just don't know what to think as there seems to be a lack of consistency and that does tend to make me nervous. The cramps continued to plague me; the ones in my hands became so bad that when I would try to eat, I would have to push both my hands down flat on the table to work the cramps out where I could hold the fork. I figure it is the leftover Sutent in my system so I know it will take a couple of months for me to feel balanced again. MRI today reveals no growth, stable disease as they call it. I am so relieved and happy, cautiously optimistic. Shelly is elated as she feels that the tumor is stable and prays for it to remain that way. I feel much more positive knowing that it is stable. I feel like I do have a fighting chance and all the positive reinforcement and thinking is truly paying off in the results. You hear the old saying that "mind over matter" is the way to go. There must be something to it because I have kept telling myself all along that I am winning this fight. I continue to fight and am looking to the future. Shelly and I have already made the decision that if the tumor grows the slightest we will immediately have our doctor contact Duke University about their immune therapy clinical trials. Shelly has all of the slides and reports ready to go in a Fed Ex package, as soon as the tumor moves, so do we. My elbows continue to bother me, leftover side effects from the Sutent I think. This has resulted in a dramatic decrease in my strength. At this time the lymph glands near my armpits seem to be growing, I will bring this to the doctor's attention at my October visit.

Shelly's Story

Larry was having so much trouble with his cramps. It started with his calves, then his feet, then his hands and finally his elbows. He could hardly pick up the gallon tea pitcher without dropping it. He could not carry or hold on to things with any kind of grip. I would see him standing beside the bed trying to get the cramps out of his legs and feet and we did a lot of midnight and early morning talking during this period of time. There were nights when Larry could not sleep; in fact that is how this book evolved and how most of it was written. We started talking about this book after the first year when people would hear our story and tell us that we ought to write a book. I tried to keep Larry Company if I didn't have work to do the next day but sometimes I had to sleep and he got up and wrote until he could come back to bed and lie down with some comfort from the cramps. I would rub his legs and feet for him. And believe it or not, when I would rub his stomach, he would just relax and go back to sleep just like a big bear.

LARRY'S TIP:

When times are hard, it is hard to concentrate on the long term. Sometimes you take life one day at a time. This is one of those times. Say it out loud. "One day at a time."

SHELLY'S TIP:

The middle of the night talks and hugging sessions are some of the best times you will ever have. There is something about the dark of night to bring a closeness that you don't find in the busy daylight hours. When the weather was good we would go outside and look at the moon and the stars, we would lie and hold each other and talk, we would laugh and we would dream. So you are tired the next day, you are loved and you are a great sense of comfort and love to your partner. Enjoy it.

COUPLE'S TIP:

Try to be respectful of each other's sleep. If your partner is too sleepy or tired to keep you company get up and go do something productive. Look at the stars, listen to the night, read a book, write in a journal, write a letter to your mother or child or spouse. If your spouse is awake with you, share the night together, pop some popcorn and talk, if your legs hurt or your hands hurt ask your partner if they could rub them for you. Tell your spouse how much you appreciate them and their friendship. You will go back to sleep after a couple of hours, if you can take a nap the next day it helps, if you can't you have to sleep and let your spouse entertain themselves for a couple of hours.

Chapter 25:
NO GROWTH!

Larry's Story

We are doing well. The results of the October MRI are no growth, stable disease. While this is great news, a part of me wants to move on to the immune therapy programs and trials. I have exhausted all chemotherapy and biotherapy trials. I want to find something to kill the cancer, I don't want to beat it back or keep it stable; I want to kill it, and I want it gone. I have been without any type of treatment for three months now and am feeling much better without the Sutent that was causing balance problems. I will wait for the next MRI in December to see if there is any growth. It is scary being off of all treatments but I feel it is the best thing for my health now. My body needs a rest; it is beat up from all the chemotherapy and biotherapy. It is a hard call when you have to start weighing quality over quantity. I don't want to be too weak to get around, I don't want to have cramps every night, I am happy being off of all the treatments except the supplements and the medications that I have to take to make sure I don't have seizures. We are now on a six-week rotation for MRIs to monitor the tumor. I feel strong and good, not sick and tired.

Shelly's Story

Our second MRI with no growth, stable disease made me very happy. I knew the first read wasn't a fluke. I know the doctors and radiologists know what they are doing but you want so badly for the tumor to remain the same or die that you just try to will it into submission. Something that we are doing is working. Blame it on the faith, the positive attitude, the love, the support, the laughter, the talks, but we are surviving. Larry is getting stronger since he is off the chemotherapy treatments, he is looking better, his hair is growing back and he acting more like his old self. No matter what seems to happen, your basic core personality comes out in times like these and I am glad to see that both Larry and I are managing through this. We are ecstatic that the tumor is still the same.

LARRY'S TIP:

When there is a victory, celebrate even if the results are "the tumor is stable, no growth." You are alive and taking an active part in your life. You are fighting against and winning one of the worst things possible to have to fight.

SHELLY'S TIP:

Take the time to live a few quiet minutes in appreciation. You have watched your spouse march through some pretty crappy treatments and procedures and they are still alive and moving up on a milestone. We wondered if Larry would be here at the two-year mark and we know he will be. Celebrate your little victories yet again.

COUPLE'S TIP:

This is the time that the cancer patient is impatient to move onto bigger and better things. They think that while the tumor or cancer is stable and they are not doing active treatments or trials that it is time to do something else. One thing you learn fast about clinical trials, the criteria can be very strict and you cannot qualify for a new clinical trial unless there is disease progression or growth. We do not have growth happening at this time. Larry and I work together to research what is out there and make sure that we are in front of the eight ball with our knowledge, not behind it. We want to remain ready for the future and be ready to select our next therapy, which will be immune therapy.

Chapter 26:
THE TERMINATORS

Larry's Story

As I write this a good friend of ours that we met at Moffitt, Bill Bartlet passed away today. His wife Julie called Shelly to let her know. We are both so sad about this loss. Bill was diagnosed 15 months ago and had been fighting the battle of his life. He also outlived the statistics and I can remember Shelly and Julie talking on the phone one night about being the first people to defeat these killer brain tumors. Did you know that the nickname of these aggressive tumors among doctors is "the terminators"? Julie was Bill's caregiver and she is devastated and lost without her partner of 12 years. You can't help but think are you next. It is unsettling to hear this kind of news as you wonder what you are doing or not that is keeping you alive. Why did he have to die? Many crazy thoughts ran through my mind about why he died and why I am still alive. We talked it over and decided to be on the safe side, we needed to go ahead and secure our funeral arrangements. No one wants to do this but we felt that it was the right thing to do as Julie told Shelly that she was so glad they had done that as it took a load off of her at the time of Bill's death. We went and shopped a couple places and decided what and where we wanted to be taken at the time of our deaths. We made arrangements for our funerals together. It was very depressing but upon getting back home and thinking about it I realized that it was one more thing that I could do to make sure Shelly isn't overwhelmed at the time of my death. I am having a sad day today over the loss of Bill and planning our funerals. Tomorrow will be better and it is okay to be sad sometimes. It is part of human nature and our feelings. It is all part of life and I have to take the bad with the good. God bless you, Brother Bill.

Shelly's story

I was sad and stunned when Julie called to tell me that Bill had died. He had been doing well up until about five days before he died when he had a hemorrhage. Those are the things that are always lurking with a brain cancer patient, hemorrhage, seizures, falls and sudden death can all occur. My heart goes out to Julie as I feel that my time will come and I get the dry heaves when I even think about Larry's death. I continue to pray to God to leave Larry with me if he could and so far he has answered that prayer and then some. God is good all the time and all the time God is good! We went to the funeral home and made our funeral arrangements. That is a strange experience to go in and plan and pay for your own funeral. Most times you die and other people handle all that business for you. I was not ready to arrange my funeral as I feel like I have lots of time but I knew it would be hard for Larry if we just went and planned his. I did not want him to feel that isolation and I felt that if we just did his I would be giving up. This way the children won't have to make those decisions. They have their own lives and families and this is one less thing that they will have to deal with in the loss of a parent. I was glad that we took control and did this as upon either one of our deaths, at least the planning is done and it makes it easier for those left behind. I think a lot more these days about those left behind.

LARRY'S TIP:

When you get bad news, like the death of a friend, grieve and do what is appropriate, whether flowers, a meal, or a visit. Work through the bad news. Try to isolate and figure out what is bothering you, what your fears are, and please share with your partner. You will both benefit if you sit together with the bad news. You have to pull yourselves together as a team and press on. You can cry and scream and get angry but then you have to dust yourself off and go forward. This is your life and you have to fight daily to keep control of it.

SHELLY'S TIP:

There will be times when you want to throw yourself down on the bed or couch and just cry. That is okay, do it if you think it will make you feel better. I found solace digging in the yard. Find your hobby and take some time for yourself. Grieve and cry for your friends, their losses and their pain. I am so glad to have met Bill and Julie as it made me feel not so alone in this battle. Whenever someone asked you what kind of cancer your husband has and you tell them brain cancer, they can't help it, they immediately gasp or show some sign of distress. When we all met in the waiting room at Moffitt and talked and got to know each other it was as if God put us together to balance and help one another. I feel like part of my balance has been removed but I will adjust and realize that we are lucky to be together and alive and we will pray for Julie's comfort and peace of mind during this tragic loss in her life.

COUPLE'S TIP:

Sometimes it is good to just hold hands or just hold each other. Words are not needed. After a period of time it will be a good idea to talk about what is bothering you even if all you can say is you are sad or feel bad. These feelings are fine, crying is fine, just don't scream at each other and take your anger out on each other. It is the cancer that is the enemy. Focus your anger on the Cancer.

Chapter 27:
SIX MONTHS AND NO GROWTH!

Larry's Story

The December MRI also shows no growth. It has now been six months with no progression. The doctor tells us to keep on doing what we are doing and we finally reveal to him that we have been doing immune supplements since the beginning. He smiles and says whatever it is keep on doing it as it sure hasn't seemed to hurt Larry, in fact it may be helping more than we know. We will now go to Moffitt every eight weeks instead of every six weeks. What a milestone when you can move your visit up two weeks and feel confident that you will be doing better. The holidays are coming up and we are in the mood to celebrate. I have made it past two years; I am feeling great and loving life. We are going to have a great visit with my parents and brother and sister. We will see Shelly's daughter and go to her house for her baby's first Christmas. It is indeed a joyous time at our house. I realize that I want to kill this tumor and I am impatient to do so. I know that the longer the tumor remains stable the longer researchers at Duke, MD Anderson and Moffitt have to work on the Phase II and Phase III immune therapy trials. They are so close to a cure, I think I may see it in my lifetime. We had a birthday party for Shelly last month and it was a real success, plenty of food, friends and fun, I gave Shelly a diamond bracelet and she loved it. I got upset today as we put out our nutcracker collection and I could not remember what they are called. I looked at Shelly and said, "The men are called?" And she said it starts with an N and I still could not recall the correct name. I called them knights, statues, but could not recall the word "nutcracker." Things like this still upset me but I realize in the big picture, I still get up, get myself dressed, try to do something productive daily, spend time with my wife and have had no tumor growth in six months. I feel like a very lucky man.

Shelly's Story:

It has been six months and no progression of the disease. You hear those words and they sound so sterile but you realize in laymen's terms you have gone six months without the beast rearing its ugly head. I am thrilled for us and so happy that Larry is feeling more confident. He is back to his old self, we don't have as much abrupt personality changes, and he is not nearly as critical and unhappy as he was back in the spring. We have had lots of talks about the personality issues, his wants and needs, my wants and needs and are doing a good job of listening to each other. The no yelling policy comes in good now when the personality is starting to change, the long-term radiation effects are starting to show up and the stress of the holidays is once again upon us. Larry and I put the decorations out and he was upset when he couldn't remember the name for the nutcrackers. We talked about it and agreed that sometimes he was going to forget things and that he could not waste time getting frustrated. We were glad to be spending another Christmas together. We take comfort in our friends; I am so happy that we are celebrating Christ's birth together this year.

LARRY'S TIP:

Doctors do not support herbal supplements, in general. I believe supplements are good and that I have been helped especially by a doctor we visited in California. Don't rule out treatments. Listen, research the information, talk to others who take herbal supplements and find out how they are doing. Stay active in your fight against cancer.

SHELLY'S TIP:

You wonder why you feel so unsettled when you have just received the best news you have had in two years. Don't look a gift horse in the mouth, don't try to analyze why him and not us. Enjoy the holidays and buy a special present for your spouse if you can afford to. It doesn't have to be anything big or expensive it just needs to be something that you know they will enjoy and will mean a lot to their heart. Spend some time thinking about a gift that will make your spouse smile.

COUPLE'S TIP:

We are now on an eight week rotation, which takes some pressure off, and gives us two more weeks between visits. We talk of the time when we will only have to go every six months. Larry wonders if this will be his last Christmas and we live it like it will be. We all hear the sayings about live life to the fullest, take it one day at a time, you only have one life, etc. You hear that when things are normal and say yeah that is what I am going to do one day. Sometimes the one day doesn't come so try to live every day like it was your last. It is amazing the things that take priority in your mind and it keeps you from getting mired in the unimportant things in life.

Chapter 28:
VANITY AND HAVING PRIDE

Larry's Story

Soon after starting radiation my hair started to fall out. I was also in the middle of chemotherapy and my spirits were somewhat low. Toward the end of the first year, I noticed a hair growing advertisement on late night television. I bought some Rogaine, read the directions and started using this following the instructions to the letter. After about a month and a half I noticed the peach fuzz beginning of hair. I continued using the Rogaine. While the hair is not thick as before cancer, I started needing to comb it and get regular haircuts. You don't feel like it but keeping up your appearance at this time is important. I was sick from the chemotherapy and bone tired from the radiation. I did not want to shave or bathe or comb my hair or anything. I didn't go out much and didn't want to. A personal issue was that I did not want to appear disabled and sick in public. I had gone to the trouble of trying to grow some hair so I decided that I should also attend to personal grooming. With Shelly's help, I began being more careful with my hygiene. I went back to shaving on a regular basis not just shaving on days when I would see the doctor or go to church. The point is to continue to take pride in your self. We think that you will feel better about yourself and your surroundings and it will reflect in your attitude and personality. In summary the caregiver or your spouse can help in this area, not to be critical but by being gentle and supportive. Shelly always has taken pictures. Photography is one of her hobbies. Checking the pictures of yourself can clearly show how other people see you. While I try to keep a handle on this, it is not always a priority especially if I get outside and start working around the yard. A positive statement by the caregiver can start the ball rolling on personal hygiene, vanity issues and future events. For example, "That is a nice shirt; it would look good at the wedding we will be going to next month."

Shelly's Story

When Larry started losing his hair it was as if he gave up on his personal hygiene and how he dressed or looked. He would be ready to go somewhere with his hair not combed, sloppy clothes on or a shirt with a stain on it. Larry would get angry and come up with a hundred excuses as to why it was okay to wear this shirt. Finally after a few sighs and huffs from Larry I asked him if we could talk about it. I explained to him that I was not being critical but that he needed to address his personal hygiene and dress. I told him that I wanted him to look clean and neat when we were in public because if I looked nice and he didn't, people would wonder why I let him go out looking so sloppy and unkempt when I knew he needed help. After this discussion Larry understood that he needed to comb his hair, brush his teeth, shave and wear clean unstained clothes when we went places. He seemed to feel better and have more pride in himself after this and sometimes he would ask me to help him pick out what he wanted to wear. It was a rough thing at first and I wanted to ask him what was he thinking dressing like that and not caring what he looked or smelled like. I wanted to smack him yet again but I realized that he was struggling with just living, much less how clean or good he looked. I would ask him how he felt before suggesting that we went anywhere and if we were going out to dinner with people I would tell him he had an hour to shower, dress and be ready so he could stop what he was doing and be ready to go on time. After we talked we were both much more aware of Larry's appearance and how he was projecting himself. You can't present an inspirational image to people if you look sloppy and haggard from not shaving.

LARRY'S TIP:

The person with cancer will no doubt be more sensitive to personal comments about hygiene. Playing a game of taking showers together and picking out each other's clothes, you select your favorite shirt of hers to wear and she selects her favorite shirt of yours for you to wear. If either person disagrees with the choice the other makes then a conversation can result in allowing each to show a preference and their opinion.

SHELLY'S TIP:

I did not want to have the hygiene conversation, I figured at age 60 Larry knew how to shave shower and dress appropriately for going out. It became apparent that his battle with cancer was tough for him and he felt sick and tired, he felt like giving up but after the conversation, he bounced back. Sometimes you have to confront embarrassing things but they need to be discussed and open communication keeps resentment and embarrassment from building up.

COUPLE'S TIP:

Personal hygiene, sex, and personal body habits are very private for every person. When you have cancer it tries to rob you of your fight and your will to live. It wreaks havoc on your body and mind. There were times when sex was out of the question, other times it is all Larry thought about, other times it just happened. Our sex life is nothing like it was before cancer but in many ways is better when it does happen and it has given us a bond to know that sex is not the main thing our marriage and lives are centered on. Talk to your spouse, make sure you are taking care of your personal hygiene, your toes and your fingernails; get pedicures if you can afford them. Pay attention to your body. You will feel 100 times better when you communicate all of these issues and work on finding something that works for both of you.

Chapter 29:
HAVING A LIMITED MEMORY

Larry's Story

It is hard to wait for the cancer to start to grow again. Fear of the unknown is very real. Life goes on and we have had a great holiday season, my second Christmas after diagnosis. I am going into my third year; odds are I won't make it through. That is the statistics talking, I choose instead to listen to myself. To continue to focus on my faith, love for my wife, happiness in feeling the sunshine and enjoying lots of good food without being sick. We have come back from Moffitt after our January check-up. The MRI reveals no growth, again. The doctor is thrilled, he tells me that I am doing better than any other patient he has. I continue to be medication-free except for the seizure pill. I have added some vitamins and a co enzyme Q10 for heart health; some doctors are recommending these for general heart health. On my MRI, the ventricles look like they are actually opening up. The right one had completely collapsed prior to the brain surgery and had always been more closed than the other one but on this MRI I could actually see they were about the same size again. The doctor and I talk and he tells me that my short term memory is not going to get any better. He says, in fact it may become worse as now the long term radiation effects are starting to show up. There isn't much data about long-term radiation effects as most people who have so much radiation are so sick that they usually don't make the two-year mark where the long-term radiation effects show up, especially when you have radiated the brain. We discussed the statistics about my chances of survival with this type of cancer. I realize that the percentage is between 2% and 15% according to which stats you read. Those are not exactly good odds but I know that I am going to continue to appreciate my life, continue my church work and being with Shelly. I am so thankful that I chose a positive road instead of a negative one as all of this would be 1,000 times harder without a good mental attitude.

Shelly's Story

We had a wonderful Christmas season and had so much fun together. We enjoyed the lights on the tree at night when it was dark, we played nice Christmas music and ate popcorn and drank wine and flavored coffee. I was so happy to make it through the season; it is bittersweet at every holiday as you wonder if this will be the last one together. I push that thought away and concentrate on helping Larry get ready for spring and summer. He has some projects he wants to do. He wants to build some stairs down into the bay, he wants to lay some sod, he has the urge to go outside and work as he is tired of winter weather and wants to be outside. The long-term radiation side effects started showing up almost to the day of the two-year mark from the beginning when radiation started. It was such a memory loss problem for Larry; I would have to tell him the same thing at least six times to get him to remember it. He was frustrated, I was frustrated, and we had great news from the doctors and behavior that didn't match. It made me crazy; he would follow me and ask me 100 questions a day. I had to constantly remind myself that he could not help it and was trying to regroup. Sometimes I would go sit outside by myself or work on some plants in the yard to have a few minutes away from the questions. We know this is a big year and we have to regroup and talk again about our hopes and fears, our plans for the future and how we were feeling emotionally. Larry had to learn to rely on himself a bit more as the questions and demands on my time were fast and furious. We had to sit down and talk at great length about how we were going to regroup and deal with the radiation effects which were to me, worse than the tumor effects.

LARRY'S TIP:

While the questions can be irritating I wanted to be current and knowledgeable. I know that at times I would ask the same question over and over but I think it helped with reinforcement. Write yourself a note; put events on a calendar so that you both keep up with what is happening. Shelly would answer the question but then would remind me that I had already asked that question. I had always asked Shelly to be honest with me when I did things like this so that I could try to be aware of what I was doing and to think before I just relied on her to do my thinking for me. Try to do your own thinking, let your partner help you work through things you don't understand. Don't struggle on your own if it truly isn't coming to your mind. Just relax and wait a bit and think about it. It will come back to you. Patience is a difficult thing to have during these times but is a must.

SHELLY'S TIP:

This was one of the most maddening times. I could not stand the constant questions; my voice was hoarse from repeating myself. I finally told Larry I felt overwhelmed by all the repetitive questions. He said he would try to not do it all day long. We regrouped, laughed about it and went on about our day. It is okay to be angry with the sick person, you are human too and your emotions are important and have to be addressed because if you emotionally fall apart you will set the tone for the future and that won't be a positive path.

COUPLE'S TIP:

Once again communication and being able to talk about how all are feeling is an important tool. You have to realize that you are two different people with two different agendas and you both have to compromise. Take some time apart if you are getting to each other. Go run an errand, do something in the dirt; it is amazing what working in the dirt does for your calm and balance. Do some kind of hobby or take a class by yourself. Everyone needs some time alone and if you talk about things no one will get their feelings hurt. You both will feel less stress because you are being honest and respectful to each other.

Chapter 30:
THE TUMOR SHRINKS!

Larry's Story

Believe it or not, my tumor is shrinking! Dr. Chowdhary says that he has rarely seen a grade III tumor shrink. The survival rate for this type of cancer is about two years or less. Here I am at the two and a half-year mark and the tumor is shrinking. Shelly and I decided to keep doing what we have been doing as it seems to be working in a most positive way on this tumor. I know that the tumor could grow somewhere else. These types of tumors give out roots with seeds, these seeds located close to the original tumor may then grow and the issues start all over again with yet another unpredictable brain tumor. The doctor indicated that there were no new growth areas at the site of the operation and the darkening of the tumor might indicate that it was dying. I hope this is true; no one can be sure. I continue to think positive thoughts and work around the house, even if I only do something for a couple of hours it helps me to feel better. On dark dreary cold days I stay indoors and read and try to rest and relax. I want to return to work at a full time job, however at this time I do not have the stamina to work full time, and I also have driving issues that would not allow me to drive to work and back on a daily basis. I am the president of the Board of Trustees at our church now, which keeps me busy. I know I don't have to do it but it is one of those things that I take pride in doing as it makes me feel that I am somehow contributing in a productive way. It can take longer to do something such as organize a meeting and review past meeting notes, but the fact that I am able to do that is unbelievable. It is now

August. My tumor has remained stable, no further shrinking but no growth. Shelly and I start to plan for my "Life Celebration Party" the party that celebrates the fact that I am still here. We have set the date for January 10. This will be a little over three years but on December 5, Shelly and I will celebrate with a nice dinner and maybe some hot tub and champagne time. I feel we deserve it and have earned the right to celebrate.

Shelly's Story

There is a lot going on in our lives now: we have helped a relative paint their house, helped some friends put in a wood floor in their daughter's new house and traveled. We have slowed down now and spend days around the house enjoying the weather and the swing in the yard. I am so happy that Larry's MRIs are showing no growth and some shrinkage of the tumor. It has been stable now for 18 months. We are so grateful to have this time together. We are going to keep on with our supplements and positive thinking. Larry doesn't much like the powered tea supplements but we feel that it is the best supplement for him at this time, it is not another pill, it is something that has seven different ingredients in it and since there are no pills involved at this time except the seizure pill we don't want to add any more pill supplements to the one. After taking 33 a day at one time Larry had grown a real hatred for taking pills. This powered tea type supplement seems to be working. Larry is actually feeling better these days and has more confidence in himself and his abilities. He has done an amazing job of fighting his way back from the cancer.

LARRY'S TIP:

A measuring project is hard for me. Can you believe that the accountant has trouble with math? The tumor is on the side of my brain that controls movement, intelligence, reasoning, behavior, memory and personality. Each lobe of the brain controls different actions. How can I have trouble with math! This is something that I have struggled with but my determination and positive attitude have helped me come to terms with the limits and I work daily to improve my brainpower. Remember the old saying "use it or lose it"? This applies now.

SHELLY'S TIP:

Keep on smiling. Enjoy this calm time in your lives. Money may be tight, and things are completely different from the way they used to be but you have grown as a person. Your compassion, understanding and empathy have expanded more than you would have ever dreamed. If you have two choices, positive or negative, you can decide which one suits you best. I have learned that negative energy makes my head hurt, it makes me feel sad and lost, and it makes me despair. I decided that the positive road is the easiest for us because you can't control the tumor but you can control your attitude.

COUPLE'S TIP:

Thank each other for all of the love and support that has brought you this far. Appreciate that you are living and happy. While you would do anything to get rid of the cancer you have learned to live with it. Some things you never get over, you learn to live with them. We are living each day as we should. We are looking at the small things and not worrying about the cancer. Sometimes days pass and it isn't even mentioned. Plan yourself celebration parties, everyone likes to eat, drink and talk. Have a few friends over to help you celebrate little victories as well as the big ones.

Chapter 31:
CONTROL OF CANCER

Larry's Story

I think that the need for support is obvious. To have control over yourself is important if you give up control of yourself, then someone else will have to take care of you and that is a burden you don't need to put onto your caregiver. They already have much more responsibility in the relationship so continue to push yourself no matter how crappy you feel to shower, dress and comb your hair. It will make you feel better even if you feel like you don't have the energy to do it. Dig deep, stay in control of your mind and your body. To defeat cancer requires the ability to challenge the medical community, the statistics and make decisions for yourself and what is in your best interests. Previously I explained that I took an experimental drug that would decrease blood to the tumor but it also decreased blood to other parts of the body. This trial was hard on me; I knew my limits by this time after two and a half years of fighting cancer. I went against what the doctor recommended and got off of that trial. I could tell it was compromising my health and stability. I also knew that it was all they had left to offer me except for the immune therapy trials that were happening at Duke University and in Los Angeles. I also knew that I would have nothing to combat the cancer; we had used the surgery, the radiation, two different kinds of chemotherapy and a biotherapy. I knew that it would be a very apprehensive time between this MRI and the next one because I didn't want to come back in six weeks to find out the tumor had doubled in size. According to the doctors when these types of tumors get out of control they can double in size in ten days. That is a scary thought. Commitment is critical. Being committed to the defeat of cancer requires that you follow doctor's orders and take your medication (I had a friend with cancer and he didn't take his medication properly; he did not last a year). But there does come a time when you as the cancer patient have to make the best decision for your health, as you know your body best. Always discuss with your doctor your feelings and if you disagree explain to the doctor why you feel this way. Cancer doctors are good at not forcing things on their patients when the patient communicates to them that they cannot handle the trial comfortably. Keep control of yourself and your care. You have a responsibility to yourself to give your cancer fight all you have.

Shelly's Story

It is so exciting to see Larry doing so well. He knows his body well enough and is tuned into it and how it feels that he is making healthy decisions for himself. He asked me how I felt about the Sutent, the biotherapy; I answered him honestly and explained to him that I felt this particular therapy was more harmful to him than the cancer. He agreed and made the decision to stop the therapy against the doctor's plan. I was proud to watch him decide for himself what he wanted to do. When we came to Moffitt the first time before the surgery Larry was so out of it that he just sat and leaned against the wall while the doctor and I talked, this time in the same examining room, he was choosing the course of action that he thought would best help him. He started writing on this book and has so much excitement and passion for this book project. We figure we are just regular people and if we can get this message out to cancer patients and their partners that there may be some tidbit in this book that can help some other couple fight through cancer. I firmly believe that Larry's "never say quit" attitude and his spirit have brought him through some pretty rotten stuff. He is happy and while we still have some memory and personality issues we continue to love and appreciate each other and are thankful for our time together. We are excited for our future. We actually feel that we have a future together for the first time in almost three years.

LARRY'S TIP:

Going to have the MRI is always stressful. I would always be apprehensive, trying to be optimistic but I could never be sure. Do something together the night before the MRI. Seeing a good comedy was always a good stress reliever. We always tried to go to bed early before MRIs in case I could not sleep and we needed to talk. We were always extra close on MRI days. Our lives could turn on one picture, one sentence: "The tumor has grown." You have to prepare for the worst and hope for the best.

SHELLY'S TIP:

When the good times are here, enjoy them. Don't feel guilty; don't wait for the other shoe to fall. Enjoy yourselves, take walks, go on picnics, and watch a movie together on the couch. The tumor is stable and so is life. We are actually reaching out and helping others and it feels good. Word gets out when something like this happens and other people find out you have gone through cancer and they call and ask for advice or just to talk. You can hear the scared in their voices, the future from diagnosis until the end can be a hard, rough road. Remember to take time for yourself as the caregiver during this time. You don't have to be on guard so much, you are back into a husband and wife relationship and it feels good. It's like losing your partner and then getting a second chance to meet and know them and love them all over again. Except this time around you are even closer as you have fought a battle together and you know that this is the person that you want to be with forever and that brings such peace and joy to your heart and soul. The closeness that we have could never be here if not for the cancer.

COUPLE'S TIP:

Celebrate any good or even neutral news. Just as there is good news, there is sometimes and will be bad news in the future. You both must prepare for it. Get your house in order. If it is already in order, recheck it. Talk to each other about the possibilities and make sure and have a positive action plan for any news especially when blood counts are low and MRIs are bad turn into positive thoughts and you will feel better. Anger is fine; it just has to be channeled correctly.

Chapter 32:
EVEN THE DOGS HAVE CANCER

Larry's Story

Our dogs. I am not making this up, but now both of our Boston terriers have cancer. Tux came to us from Boston Rescue sick with cancer already. They called us up and said, "Can you please take him, we can't think of anyone else who could identify with this guy." We loved him from day one. He was a great dog; he loved people and knew he was sick but kept on anyway. We discovered knots on the outside of his stomach about 3 months after he came to live with us. We took him to the vet, had the knots removed and three months later he started coughing. The findings were not good, his cancer has spread into the lymph nodes around his throat and it was cutting off his airway. We gave him medication to try to help but nothing did the job. We had to put him to sleep and it was a sad, sad, day. Imagine how the death of a dog from cancer sent me spinning. I wondered was I next just like with Bill? I know a person and a dog do not compare but the feeling is the same. I didn't want death around me; I didn't want it to know my name or where I was. We buried him in the backyard under an azalea bush and we miss him very much. Sam, our Boston that we have had for five years, passed away as well. Sam and Tux died three weeks apart. Sam had liver cancer, two masses on his liver and his liver quit functioning. The medicine didn't work and he had no energy to eat or get up or play. We took him in and the vet told us that it was time to let Sam go as he was in pain and not doing well. We cried all the way home from the vet, and then we struggled when we got home to bury Sam next to Tux. We miss them. Sam was a good friend to me.

Shelly's Story

Cancer seems to be everywhere; I have a husband and two dogs and all with cancer. I gave out pills twice a day to all the boys, Sam, Tux and Larry. I would have to feed Sam and Tux separately as they had different medications and I could not let one eat the other's food. We would do this in the a.m. and p.m. and then I would say "Larry, have you taken your pills?" We knew when Tux came to live with us that he had cancer and might not live long but Larry and I decided to give him a good, kind loving home the last days that he had. He fit right in, it was like he knew Larry was sick and he was a great companion to him and Sam. I would come through the living room some days and there would be Larry, Tux and Sam all piled up in Larry's recliner and all snoring, and not in sync I might add. I have pictures of them and they are priceless. I was so sad to put Tux to sleep but realized that we had given him six months of squirrel chasing, good eating and a family to love him. When Sam was diagnosed with the liver problems I went automatically into denial and thought I could keep him going with medications. He lasted another two months and then became sick and in pain, Tux had died three weeks earlier and I knew that the right thing to do was to put him to sleep as well. My heart was breaking and I really felt the pressure of cancer involved in the things that I loved. I told myself that it was okay, we were all doing the best we could and death is a part of life. We don't want to think about it but when you realize that it can be closer than you think you have to keep your mind on the positive and don't let the sadness scare you.

LARRYíS TIP:

I was sad and could not help it. I knew the cancer issues with Tux and was able to anticipate. Sam was harder due to our long-term relationship. Did God ordain this? Why Sam? He had always had a hard life as a rescue dog until he came to live with us. There are things that happen that we ask why and receive no answer. I miss Sam; I miss my buddy, at times like these I just have to be thankful that I had Sam at all.

SHELLY'S TIP:

Larry and I enjoyed taking care of Tux and he provided us with lots of smiles and laughs. We were lucky to have him with us for six months. Sam was a greater loss and I worried how Larry would take it but he seemed to be okay. Sad but okay. When sadness seems to be camping out on your doorstep remember that you have permission to grieve but remember the happy times as well. I can't bring them back, I miss them but I can be grateful that I had the pleasure of knowing them at all. Once again, the old "be thankful for what you do have instead of what you don't have".

COUPLE'S TIP:

We were a little depressed during this period of time. We loved our dogs, they traveled with us, we stayed at home with them and we were all used to hanging out together. It was back to just the two of us again and we were grateful that we had the chance to have the dogs and to be able to help the rescue with them as where would they have ended up if we had said no. Sometimes when you are at your worst, the best thing to do is reach out and help someone or something else and it will, believe it or not, help you.

Chapter 33:
GAINING CONTROL

Larry's Story

With a brain tumor there seem to be issues and action needed on a daily basis. Sometimes we have projects that take longer than I hoped. When something gets accomplished, a medical milestone, celebrate the victories. When Bill Bartlet died of cancer I was so sad but I knew I must get past the death and fight on. Cancer doesn't take any holidays, sick time or PTO; cancer has no conscience and doesn't care how you feel. Sometimes I don't feel like it, but if I want to live I have to fight on. Sometimes I force myself to be positive when it would be so easy just to slip into the negative, forcing the positive is harder but it also lets me know I am still alive and in control of my thoughts and body. I continue to be active and continue to think of ways that I could go back to work. I am an accountant by trade and I just don't think that I need to go back and try to do important tax work until my brain is ready. I focus on the positive of being able to do taxes again. There was a time when I could not even sign my name so I am proud of myself and pat myself on the back for the job I am doing to stay active. That is my job for now and I am grateful to have it. I am in control of what happens. My attitude will help me to survive the sorrows and pitfalls of this adventure called cancer.

Shelly's Story

We continue to adjust to life with cancer. We have learned to live with our limits and really appreciate life in general now. We are coming up on the three-year mark. I work in the yard, Larry works on his projects around the house, he continues to read, and he says he thinks that even if he is a slow reader that the reading helps makes his mind sharper. I agree with that. He is more like himself and I love his sense of humor and fighting spirit. Sometimes I want to put him on my shoulders like they did in the movie *"Rudy"* the walk-on player that had no physical strength but enough heart to move a team of big burley Notre Dame Football players. I want to run around the yard carrying him and going "Larry, Larry, Larry" as his spirit is something that I will forever cherish about him and something that I am grateful to be a part of. His attitude rubs off on you and you can't help but smile when he jokes around with you.

LARRY'S TIP:

Trying to return to normal will be in steps. I practice math often, and I keep a close eye on the checkbook. Shelly told me that one of the things that tipped her off that something was wrong was that I put the payroll deposit in one bank and wrote the payroll checks from another and bounced 27 checks two days before they found the tumor. I don't ever want to do that type of thing again so I make sure I get printouts from the bank and don't rush through balancing the checkbook. Rely on your partner to help you, check your work. The more of your own affairs that you can handle the better you feel. No one wants to feel as if they have lost control of their life. I don't think I can ever work in an office environment again as my bosses will not appreciate my falling asleep often, nor my short term memory issues when working on a big project.

SHELLYíS TIP:

Try to be flexible. By now you have learned to live with cancer believe it or not, and you have learned that being panicky and scared only hurts you. I like being positive, no one can do it all the time but we are amazed at the way positive thinking, faithfulness and love have enhanced our lives. We don't take the newspaper and watch limited news as most of the media today has nothing but negative issues to show and just like being positive, being too negative gets old. Positive and negative thoughts go through my mind daily. I have learned to get my worry list down to three items, think about them, if I can fix something on one I will, if not I let it drop off the list and add another one of my worries. I cannot save the world, I cannot save Larry, I cannot cure cancer but I can fight to the bitter end and believe that we will prevail. Don't give up. Don't let the negative thoughts drag you down. Once again be thankful for what you do have, not what you don't have. Practice this thought daily. Try the three worries list. It works and helps you to identify how you deal with things which will only help you in the future.

COUPLE'S TIP:

Be thankful for what you have, while you cannot forget the bad things learn from them and think about any ways to turn a negative into a positive. Take a walk, talk to each other, go visit a neighbor, call some friends and ask them to bring potluck and come over for dinner. People love to see you succeeding especially when their support is part of the reason you are successful in your fight against cancer.

Chapter 34:
THREE YEARS AND
COUNTING

Larry's Summary

Guess what? I made it! I have passed the dreaded three-year mark. It has now been three years two months and ten days since diagnosis. I am feeling good. We are now in the final stages of writing this book. Instead of writing about a specific event or issue in this chapter I am stepping back to try and summarize and touch upon some of the more general issues of the past three years and some things that I have learned and want to share with you. My cancer has been stable for 22 months now. The last MRI in December showed that the tumor was stable, the same size but also darker on the images. I asked the doctor if it could be something to do with the equipment and he answered no, that most of my MRIs were done on the same machine. I asked him in his experience when an image on the MRI starts to darken and fade what does it suggest? The doctor looked at me and again at the MRI and said this is typically an indication that the growth is dying. The doctor quickly moved on and said that this was by no means a medical opinion but an observation. We decided that future MRIs would provide more information and that today the tumor remains stable and that was good enough for us. Friends will give you the "I feel sorry for you" look and ask "How are you doing?" I make it a point to answer in a positive way and then I ask them how they are doing? Some say okay but many are taken off guard when I answer the question and then fire a question right back. I always stop moving and listen for the answer. We don't listen to each other very well in today's world. Everyone is in such a rush, and you would be surprised at the answers you receive when you listen. Listen and see that other families and individuals have issues and problems; therefore I am not the only person with problems. There is often an opportunity to empathize with the friend and make a positive statement. Only takes a minute to do this. I don't allow myself or others to feel sorry for me. No pity parties. Instead my conversation goes to accomplishments, such as being able to get back into tax work plus the work we have put into remodeling the house. I am proud to be the president of the Board of Trustees at church. I am proud that I can still be productive and that the quality of life is good. I spend good quality time with my wife, my family, my friends and myself. I appreciate this second chance that I have been provided with and hope that I will continue to use it to be a positive and inspirational person to others, especially those who battle cancer. Sex was always important to me but the past three years have changed that as well. While I don't have as much sex as I would like I still have sex and it is still good. We have undergone big changes in our relationship, marriage, friendships, financial status and just about any other thing you can think of. This illness hit us fast and hard with no mercy. We adapted to it, decided to be positive and faithful to ourselves and others. We thanked our God for all the things that he has in store for us for our future and we continue to press on and keep fighting, I want to be here 5, 10, 20 years from now. I have learned to be at peace with my surroundings and myself. I have learned to be positive in the face of large negative odds. Two percent is about as bad as it gets. These are not the kind of odds that you can usually win against but I have learned to fight because I am worth it. I want to be here and I want to go in front of people and be a motivational speaker for fighting cancer. I want a cure for cancer in my lifetime and I am going to do everything that I can to help in the fight to stomp cancer out.

Chapter 35:
THE CELEBRATION OF LIFE

Larry and Shelly's story

We write this after the "Life Celebration Party." What a wonderful party even if we did host it. We ordered Italian food, had it catered in, and we had a huge chocolate cake with chocolate frosting and lots of fresh, hot bread. There were 86 people at the party. We had such a good time, it was great to see all of these people again, some after three years, they had kept up via email, phone calls and cards and letters. Two of the three doctors that managed care came to the party and brought their wives. They toasted Larry and Shelly and told those in attendance what a special patient Larry was to them and how they felt he was going to live on for a long time. It was wonderful to hear and to celebrate with all of those who had a part in our fight against cancer. We took Larry's picture with each friend that came and Shelly also had a book for everyone to sign so that they could give Larry their own message about his fight with cancer. The book is amazing and will be a priceless memory in the future. The word that kept coming up over and over in the signed book was "inspiration," which makes us feel good as that is what we want to spread, Inspiration and hope; faith and love, all the things that we all want but sometimes struggle to achieve. We are all here together and we get wrapped up in our own lives and time just goes by and you never quite get to do what you wanted after all. We feel blessed to have learned that while we will all one day pass on, the time here is special and when you are given a death sentence and somehow survive it you have to feel that somebody is looking out for you. We thank God for leaving Larry here for a while to live in peace and happiness with his Shelly. Please try to not let pain, anger and depression rule you. Sometimes life is not fair, I don't think any of us was promised an easy life and when you get life altering news it is painful and frightening. Don't let these emotions rob you of the energy and strength that you will need to keep yourself happy, at peace and staying alive.

Chapter 36:
A NEW ENDING
TO THE BOOK

Larry's Story

After the celebration of life party we planned to end the book, but a new ending to the book has been provided by Jesus. At my previous appointment in December the doctor noted that the tumor was somewhat darker. I asked why the tumor was darker and could it be due to a different MRI machine? He said "no, that all machines were calibrated the same". He then said that "from my experience when a tumor gets darker it is getting ready to explode with growth or it is dying. When you have the next MRI at the end of April we will know what is going on. I really don't want to comment any further". As the next MRI approached in April I was my usual nervous and apprehensive self about the results. It was a considerable amount of time before the doctor came into the examination room. This makes you even more anxious. When Dr. Chowdhary entered the room he was all smiles, he said "Larry, you have won the Super Bowl"! The tumor is dead! The only evidence of the tumor is the scar tissue"! Shelly and I were both elated and light headed to the point of being giddy. As I write this; I can't help but think about the last 3 and one half years. First, my God who was always with me during this fight, second, my wife, who without her care I would not have survived, third, my church and all of the support by helping out at our house during trying times, fourth, the doctors which are pictured in the book and neighbors like Bill Pearce and Tony Barberi who carried me when I could not walk. I have beaten this tumor! I have won! I have walked through the hell of it all and survived. God truly does have a mission for me and I can't wait to go out and do his bidding.

Shelly's Story

I was ready to go to Moffitt this time. I was apprehensive about the results as I wanted to tumor to be gone from our lives. I wanted us to get on with life without the tumor and look to our future and helping others with the cancer battle. When you spend a lot of time with neuro oncologists you come to realize that they do serious business on a daily basis and that they are constantly under the gun to find a way to control and stop these terrible brain tumors. To see a neuro oncologist practically dancing into a room is a sight to behold. He was so happy to inform us that the tumor had died and all that was left behind was scar tissue. To be able to go from a MRI and doctor visit every six weeks to six months now is in itself a miracle. We no longer have to live with the tumor. We will not get back what we have lost, however, we won't loose any more. The burden that was lifted off of us on this bright sunshine day in May was like being given a second chance to have a life together. Without our faith, determination, respect and love for one another I feel that this fight would have ended differently. I feel like the luckiest person on the face of the planet and I know that no matter what comes my way in the future that I am strong enough and faithful enough to work my way through it to victory.

LARRY'S TIP:

I must dedicate this tip to Jesus. My actual summary comments are in chapter 35. I don't know of many people who have rid themselves of a brain tumor or having a happy ending to a brain tumor. If I can fight my way through this, you can too. Several friends have called since the news of the tumor to tell me how grateful to God they are and they feel that I have a mission and a vision. I will wait for Jesus to call upon me and meanwhile remember the question, "What are you living for"?

SHELLY'S TIP:

All I can say is we have a different road to walk. Remember the voice on the porch that told me to "be at peace my child, the outcome will not be as they say it is?" I do. No doubt in my mind that God's hand was all over this one and you need to never forget that when you are at your lowest, he is at your side. The tumor is behind us and we have a bright future ahead. We both know that anything can happen in the blink of an eye and change your world. We want to be here to speak to others about our journey with cancer, to help others, to spread the word about inspiration and faith and to love and be together in sickness and health as long as we both shall live. We thank God for his blessings and we are going forth to do his bidding. We will keep on loving and respecting each other and we shall always keep the faith. God is good all the time!

COUPLE'S TIP:

We are thankful for the news of no tumor. Shelly will start nursing school in August and will have the opportunity to make a small difference to other's who are fighting cancer. Larry will work on marketing the book and raise money for cancer research utilizing our non for profit "Bevis Cancer Foundation". We have received our EIN number already. If you would like information about the Bevis Cancer Foundation or if you would like to talk to someone don't hesitate to call us at 850-916-4930 or email us at: wildflower9@mchsi.com or our address: 4986 Hickory Shores Blvd, Gulf Breeze, FL 32563.

The Doctors

I would like to make a summary statement about the doctors responsible for my being here today. Thank you to Dr. Steven Brem for his wonderful surgical skills, Dr. Ken Long for his humbleness and for his kindness and his ability to always be available to us in the beginning when things were so uncertain and scary. One time I was out in the yard and Dr. Long was out riding his bicycle, he stopped and had some water with me and I will always remember how athletic and young he looked riding off on his bicycle that day with a big smile and a positive attitude. He just wanted to stop by and see how I was doing. For Dr. Frank Andrews who was more like a manager. He would receive all the reports as the oncologist. We would talk weekly about medications, what worked what didn't. He was a good listener and also very smart and experienced. For Dr. Mark Chamberlin who helped me through the first two years, for Dr. Chowdhary who is my doctor at Moffitt Cancer Center in Tampa, Florida. He is a coach. We talk about my current therapy, and we discuss future possible programs and trials. He does not hurry us. He also has a very competent staff that always has our best interest at heart, my sincerest thanks to these gentlemen who give time and talent in trying to find the cure for cancer. I owe my life to your care and for that I will always be grateful.

To all the readers:

Thank you for taking the time to read this book, we hope you gained something from the story of our adventure with cancer. We hope you will take some comfort, inspiration, laughter or understanding from this book.

God's Speed............

Larry and Shelly Bevis

One half of the proceeds of any book sale or motivational speech fee will go into the Bevis Cancer Foundation to help with the fight against cancer.

COUPLES ANSWERS FOR CANCER

How to fight and survive to defeat
cancer as a couple

By: Larry and Shelly Bevis

Author Biography

LARRY BEVIS grew up in Peoria, IL and moved to Florida in 1997. He retired and started teaching school at the college level Part time at the local Community College. He is a cancer survivor and currently marketing and speaking with people who are interested in defeating cancer while living a joyful life. He has founded the "Bevis Cancer Foundation" with half of the proceeds from any book sale or motivational speech going to the "Bevis Cancer Foundation" to help combat cancer research. He currently resides in Gulf Breeze Florida and is looking forward to writing his next book with many cancer patients involved in writing their stories. He and Shelly have been married for five years.

SHELLY BEVIS grew up in North Alabama and moved to Florida in 2003. She and Larry met believe it or not in the paint department at the local Wal-Mart. Shelly has two girls, and 3 grandchildren with two on the way. She enjoys spoiling her grandchildren, gardening, and reading and is currently going to school to become an RN with oncology as a specialty. She hopes to make a difference in people's lives that battle cancer. She also resides in Gulf Breeze Florida and is looking forward to becoming a Registered Nurse.